HISTORY OF SPORTS

HOCKEY

BY JOHN F. WUKOVITS

Lucent Books, Inc.
San Diego, California

Titles in The History of Sports Series include:
  Baseball
  Basketball
  Football
  Golf
  Hockey
  Soccer

Library of Congress Cataloging-in-Publication Data

Wukovits, John F., 1944–
    Hockey / by John F. Wukovits.
        p.   cm. — (History of sports)
    Includes bibliographical references (p.) and index.
    ISBN 1-56006-745-4
    1. Hockey—Juvenile literature. [1. Hockey.] I. Title. II. Series.
GV847.25 .W85   2001
796.962—dc21   00-011220

Contents

FOREWORD

MORE THAN MANY areas of human endeavor, sports give us the opportunity to see the possibilities in our physical selves. As participants, we all too quickly find limits in how fast we can run, how high we can jump, how far and straight we can hit a golf ball. But as spectators we can surpass those limits as we view the accomplishments of others and see how fast, how smooth, and how strong a human being can be. We marvel at the gravity-defying leaps of a Michael Jordan as he strains towards a basketball hoop or at the dribbling of a Mia Hamm as she eludes defenders on the soccer field. We shake our heads in disbelief at the talents of a young Tiger Woods hitting an approach shot to the green or the speed of a Carl Lewis as he appears to glide around an Olympic track.

These are what the sports media call "the oohs and ahhs" of sports—the stuff of highlight reels and *Sports Illustrated* covers. But to understand a sport only in the context of its most artistic modern athletes is shortsighted, for it does little justice to the accomplishments of the athlete *or* to the sport itself. Far more wise is to view a sport as a continuum—a constantly moving, evolving process. On this continuum are not only the superstars of today, but the people who first played the sport, who thought about rules and strategies that would make it more challenging to play as well as a delight to watch.

Lucent Books' series, *The History of Sports,* provides such a continuum. Each book explores the development of a sport, from its basic roots onwards, and tries to answer questions that a reader might wonder about. Who were its first players and what sorts of rules did the sport have then? What kinds of equipment were used in the beginning and what changes have taken place over the years?

Each title in *The History of Sports* also identifies key individuals in the sport's history—people whose leadership or skills have made a difference in the way the sport is played today. Included will be the easily recognized names, the Mia Hamms and the Sammy Sosas, the Wilt Chamberlains and the Wilma Rudolphs. But there are also the names of past greats, people like baseball's King Kelly, soccer's Sir Stanley Matthews, and basketball's Hank Luisetti—who may be less familiar today, but were as synonymous with their sports at one time as the "oohs and ahhs" players of today.

Finally, the series looks at the aspects of a sport that are particularly important in its current point on the continuum. Baseball today is better understood knowing about salary caps and union negotiators. One cannot truly know modern soccer without knowing about the specter of fan violence at matches. And learning about the role of instant replay is critical to a thorough understanding of today's professional football games. In viewing a sport as a continuum, the strides that have been made along the way are that much more admirable. It is a richer view, and one that shows how yesterday's limits have been surpassed—and how the limits of today are the possibilities of athletes in the future.

From Canada to the World

THIRTY YEARS AGO, a history of sports would not have included the game of ice hockey, more simply known as hockey. The standard sports would certainly have appeared: Baseball and Babe Ruth would have vied for attention with football and Knute Rockne, the famed Notre Dame coach. Hockey, though, would have been relegated to the back pages, occupying space with the other lesser-known sports like handball and wrestling.

That has changed, however, as hockey enjoyed phenomenal growth in the latter part of the twentieth century. From its beginnings in Canada, the sport spread throughout North America, Europe, and Asia to become one of the most profitable businesses in the sporting world. Its popularity, which never wavered in Canada but endured ups and downs in the United States, has never been greater.

What produced such a dramatic situation that fans in nations already absorbed with other sports would make time for yet another? One factor was television. Just as television has become an integral part of the political and entertainment worlds, so did the medium affect hockey. Beginning in the 1950s, television beamed broadcasts of hockey games into the homes of families who would never have been able to view a game otherwise, either because they lived too far from one of the ice arenas or they resided in an area in which hockey was not yet popular. Television introduced the game to the spectator who had previously been unfamiliar with it.

A second factor that boosted hockey's popularity was the mobility of its fans. For the first six decades of the twentieth century, in the United States at least, professional hockey existed only in the Midwest and Northeast. Four professional teams—Detroit, New York, Boston, and Chicago—developed extensive followings. When some of these sports fans moved from one of the four cities to areas that had no hockey, they took their love of the game with them. Although they had to endure years, even decades, without professional hockey, they maintained the

hope that one day the sport would spread across the nation. When it did, they were there to support it.

Hockey received a tremendous boost in the United States in 1980 when the American Olympic squad pulled off one of sports' greatest upsets on their way to garnering the hockey gold medal. In their quest, they defeated the mighty Soviet Union team, a potent conglomeration of talent that led most observers to assume that the gold medal was theirs for the taking. A unit of unknowns from the United States had other plans, how-

Hockey has enjoyed unprecedented popularity throughout the world since the latter part of the twentieth century.

ever, and people from Maryland to California, from Montana to Texas, were caught up in the hockey fever that swirled about the triumphant young men. Al Michaels, a sportscaster broadcasting the exciting game, asked his viewers as the final seconds ticked off, "Do you believe in miracles?"[1] The American people answered in the affirmative, and hockey was off and running in the United States.

A sport that had thrived only in the Midwest and Northeast now became a national sport. Expansion brought professional teams to California and Texas, Florida and Colorado. Youth leagues flourished in North Dakota prairie towns and Appalachian Mountain cities. At any time during the year, school-age youth played ice hockey, in-line hockey, or both.

The Same Features as Any Other Sport

As a result of this growth, hockey now occupies a place with other major sports. Rightfully so, for its history offers people and events just as exciting as those of its counterparts. Howie Morenz, Maurice "Rocket" Richard, Gordie Howe, Bobby Orr, and Wayne Gretzky command the same respect and awe as Joe DiMaggio and Ty Cobb receive in baseball and Michael Jordan and Kareem Abdul-Jabbar enjoy in basketball. Babe Ruth's sixty home runs for years were the measure of greatness in hitting; Richard's fifty goals in fifty games

were likewise the yardstick of excellence in hockey.

The fabled teams of hockey's history match those talented squads offered by other sports. The Montreal Canadiens of the late 1950s equaled in talent the 1927 New York Yankees' "Murderers Row." Gordie Howe's Detroit Red Wing dynasty of the early 1950s produced as much drama as Joe Montana's football championship teams. In the 1980s, Wayne Gretzky's Edmonton Oilers skated past opponents in the same way that Bill Russell's Boston Celtics dominated basketball teams in the 1950s.

Like other big-time sports, hockey has had its dramatic moments that stir emotions. According to legend, Babe Ruth once told a youth he would hit a home run for him. In hockey's counterpart, the Toronto Maple Leafs vowed not to disappoint a Toronto schoolgirl by losing the postseason championship. Lou Gehrig said goodbye to baseball in an emotional speech at Yankee Stadium; Gordie Howe departed after playing on the same professional team with his two sons.

Today, hockey enjoys a level of popularity similar to that of baseball, football, and basketball. Young people attend school dressed in hockey jerseys and hang posters of hockey stars on their bedroom walls. What had once been Canada's sport has now been taken over by much of the world. As such, hockey deserves a prominent place in the history of sports.

CHAPTER 1

"Good Fun May Be Expected"

A S IS TRUE of most sports, the beginnings of hockey are shrouded in uncertainty. Although many nations lay claim to the sport, most observers believe that hockey, at least as it is known today, started in Canada. Other than in the Olympic Games and other amateur tournaments, hockey largely remained a Canadian pastime until the 1960s. At that time it exploded in popularity to become an international sport.

European Origins

Several European nations contend that ice hockey evolved from the popular game of field hockey, a contest in which residents of various villages flooded to nearby fields to battle for area supremacy and for the honor of their towns. In France, athletes used a wooden stick, called *hoquet*, which resembled a shepherd's crook, and batted a ball about the fields.

The Irish claim that the sport originated from their game called hurling, which used sticks and balls. A seventeenth-century Dutch painting depicts athletes skating on ice and smacking at a flat rock. In Russia near the end of the same century, skaters played a similar game but used a ball instead of a rock.

While some of those claims are more credible than others, no one denies that British skaters played a game on ice in the 1800s. One account tells of an 1853 game at Windsor Castle, the home of the British royal family, in which young men grabbed sticks, headed to a nearby frozen pond, and hit a wooden barrel plug back and forth as Queen Victoria watched. In 1899, British athletes traveled to Russia to play a team from St. Petersburg on the frozen Neva River.

Canadian Origins

Different Canadian locales boast of being the birthplace of Canadian hockey. Some authorities believe that an 1810 college game on Long Pond in Windsor, Nova Scotia, was the first hockey contest played in Canada, an account supported by a former student's 1870s recollection of his time at King's Collegiate in which he reminisced about a game similar to hockey: "The Devil's Punch Bowl and the Long Pond, back of the college, were favorite resorts, and we used to skate in winter, on moonlight nights, on the ponds. I recollect John Cunard having his front teeth knocked out with a hurley [stick] by Pete Delancey of Annapolis."[2]

English soldiers imported the game to Canada in the 1800s when they were stationed in the cold reaches of North America. Because there were thousands of frozen rivers, lakes, and ponds and millions of trees providing branches for sticks, the soldiers idled their spare moments in a spirited game, containing few rules, in which they batted a ball with the sticks. An 1855

story mentions a match in Kingston, Ontario, among soldiers of Her Majesty's Royal Canadian Rifles who gathered field hockey sticks and a lacrosse ball and played on the frozen harbor behind their barracks.

Another version credits the invention of hockey to students at McGill University in Montreal who started playing a game in the 1870s that took elements from field hockey, lacrosse, and rugby. Skating to the "McGill Rules," created by J. G. A. Creighton, nine players per side competed in front of an audience at Victoria Ice Rink on March 3, 1875. The Montreal *Gazette* recorded that

There is great debate as to the origins of hockey in Canada.

Good fun may be expected, as some of the players are reported to be exceedingly expert at the game. Some fears have been expressed on the part of the attending spectators that accidents are likely to occur through the ball [puck] flying about in a too-lively manner to the imminent danger of onlookers.[3]

In the 1880s, Kingston supported the first official hockey league of four teams, who competed on outdoor rinks. These rinks were surrounded by a one-foot-tall plank to stop the pucks, flat wooden disks that had replaced the ball, from sliding away. Players skated up the ice with a flourish and a shower of ice shavings as they attempted to shove the puck between two upright poles protruding from the ice. Since the poles were not connected by a crossbar and sported no net, the players could score from either in front of or behind the posts. Frequently, the player, puck, and goaltender wound up in a tangled heap on one side of the crossbar or the other.

From the game's early beginnings, hockey quickly spread to other portions of Canada. Two clubs were organized in Montreal and one in Toronto, and winter carnivals included hockey tournaments in their roster of activities. The first major championship contest occurred at the 1883 Montreal Winter Carnival, where McGill University continued its early dominance of the sport.

City leagues enhanced the opportunity to play and watch hockey, since travel time and

THE McGILL RULES

J. G. A. Creighton's rules gave hockey some structure that it had not enjoyed before. Drawing from rugby, lacrosse, and field hockey, Creighton stipulated the following:
- There are nine players per side.
- The game is over when three goals have been scored.
- A referee will maintain order.
- Fighting shall receive a major penalty.

costs in those days made it difficult for teams from different communities to engage each other. The Montreal City Hockey League pitted four local teams against one another. Gradually, the idea of matching star teams from different towns gained popularity, which by the 1880s resulted in some cities constructing ice arenas. Amateur hockey gained momentum with these steps. In 1886, the Amateur Hockey Association of Canada was founded, the first formal group in the country designed to promote amateur hockey and "protect it from professionalism and to promote the cultivation of kindly feeling among the members of hockey clubs."[4]

Other leagues soon arose in Canada, including the Ontario Hockey Association, which attempted to further the sport in that province. Unlike infant versions of many sports, such as rugby and football, which seemed to bring out rowdy fans, early hockey appealed to society's upper crust. Finely dressed men and women attended games, chatted about their daily business ventures, and ate sumptuous meals between hockey periods. The game became an "event" at which prominent people loved to be seen. Although they may have come from the so-called upper classes, the spectators warmed to the speed and violence that seemed to be an integral part of hockey.

The Rules of the Game

These early contests contained few formal rules, with each community drawing up its own set of regulations. An organization in the 1870s created the Halifax Rules, which required stones to mark the goal areas and stated that the puck could not be lifted in the air and that sticks had to be kept below the shoulders. The McGill Rules, codified by students from the university, adopted the

Halifax Rules and added other features, such as setting the length of the match at two thirty-minute halves, assigning referees to maintain control, and introducing penalties to reduce fighting.

In 1879 the vulcanized rubber puck was formally adopted as part of the game. Players found it easier to control than the lighter wooden puck. The harder rubber disk was also less likely to jump off sticks and fly into the spectator area.

At first, nine men played per side, but the number dropped to seven in the mid-1880s—a goaltender to stop opposing shots on the goal area, two defensemen to help keep the opposing team away from the goal area, three forwards to take the attack to the opposing goal area, and a rover who played either offense or defense. Around the same

Hockey's earliest competitions had few formal rules.

time, posts protruding from the ice replaced the rocks to denote goal areas.

The idea for a net attached to the posts came in 1899. According to legend, a player walking along a pier studied fishermen gathering fish with their nets and decided that a net could stop pucks from going all over. On January 6, 1899, a net connecting the goalposts was used for the first time by the Halifax Wanderers and Crescent club.

This improvement helped, but it still posed problems. Sometimes the netting was stretched so tightly from post to post that the puck hit it and bounced back before the referee could determine if a goal had been scored. The wide holes in the netting also permitted pucks to speed right through. Ottawa Senators goalie Percy LeSueur designed a new net in 1912 that used crossbars for the first time to connect the poles. The

THE NUMBERS VARY

In the early days of hockey, each team put nine players on the ice. The number dropped to seven in the late 1880s after a club participating in the Montreal Winter Carnival arrived two men short. Showing excellent sportsmanship, the opposing team agreed to play with only seven men, and over a period of time, athletes found that the smaller number offered more freedom of maneuver and added excitement to the game. When the National Hockey League started in 1917, it dropped the seventh player and standardized the number of men on the ice at six. That number has remained constant ever since.

modern version, which sports a semicircular netting that traps pucks shot from in front, was commonly used by 1927.

At first, athletes, including the goaltenders, wore only short shin pads, since the puck was always propelled along the ice's surface and never lifted into the air. Goaltenders, also called goalies, often shoved fur down the front of their pant legs to create improvised pads for their shins. The goalies used the same sticks as the other players—short, curved sticks—and everyone wore uniforms consisting of turtleneck sweaters and knitted wool caps.

The first games permitted no forward passing. The game instead relied on one athlete controlling the puck, skating down the ice toward the opposing goal area, and trying to propel the puck past the goalie. Little strategy governed the play; one side rushed the other and tried to score, then the other side did the same in reverse.

The game started when a referee placed the puck on the ice and arranged two opposing players' sticks on either side. As he slowly backed away, he shouted "Play!" indicating when both athletes could start swiping at the puck to gain possession. The vicious swinging resulted in bruises and injuries to referees' legs, so the rules were changed to allow referees to toss the puck between opposing players, similar to the modern method of starting play.

The early game included many tough contests between rugged teams. Long-standing rivalries among cities translated to violence on the ice, a problem that has plagued the sport ever since. In one 1905 game between the Rat Portage Westerners and the Ottawa Capitals, the referee wore a hard hat for protection, and fans cheered in delight whenever a player "accidentally" knocked it off his head. The first recorded death in the sport occurred in 1907, when Owen McCourt of Cornwall was hit over the head with a stick. He was rushed to a hospital, but died the next morning. Charles Masson of the Ottawa Vics was charged with murder, but a sympathetic jury acquitted him of the charges.

Originally purchased for $48, the Stanley Cup is professional hockey's most coveted prize.

The Stanley Cup

Hockey took a huge step toward respectability and importance in 1892 when the governor general of Canada, Frederick Arthur, Lord Stanley of Preston, purchased a silver trophy cup for $48 and awarded it to the winner of an annual playoff between amateur clubs. Lord Stanley, an avid sportsman and a future prime minister of Great Britain, wanted to promote amateur hockey throughout the nation, and he believed that government sponsorship of the Stanley Cup, as it is reverently known today, would achieve that purpose. As intended, the cup could be contested by champions of various leagues. Lord Stanley's cup was one of the first major steps transforming hockey into Canada's national pastime.

Lord Stanley announced his new prize at a March 18, 1892, banquet hosted by the Ottawa Amateur Athletic Club: "I have for some time past been thinking that it would be a good thing if there were a challenge cup which should be held from year to year by the champion hockey team in the dominion."[5]

The initial Stanley Cup match occurred in Montreal on March 22, 1894, between the Montreal Amateur Athletic Association and the Ottawa Capitals. Played before five thousand fans, Montreal swept to victory and gained possession of the first Stanley Cup. A

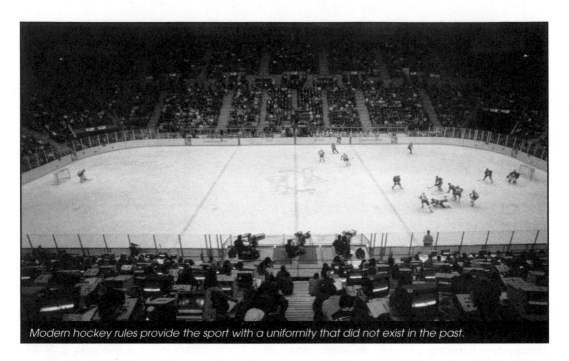
Modern hockey rules provide the sport with a uniformity that did not exist in the past.

Montreal newspaper account of the historic match reported,

> The hockey championship was decided here tonight, and never before in the history of the game was there such a crowd present at a match or such enthusiasm evinced. There were fully 5,000 persons at the match, and tin horns, strong lungs and a general rabble predominated. The ice was fairly good. The referee forgot to see many things. The match resulted in favor of Montreal by three goals to one.[6]

For seventeen years amateur squads competed for the Stanley Cup, but a new game lurked on the horizon. Lord Stanley hoped to establish the amateur version throughout Canada, but hockey would gain its greatest popularity on the backs of professionals— men who played the game for money. In 1910 the Stanley Cup was awarded to the top professional squad, and today, the trophy—the same one purchased by Lord Stanley over a century ago—is awarded to the National Hockey League (NHL) team who wins each year's Stanley Cup playoffs.

Today's Rules

The modern game of hockey as played in the NHL now offers a uniformity that did not exist in 1910. A regulation ice hockey rink is two hundred feet long and eighty-five feet wide and has rounded corners. To protect spectators from errant pucks, four-foot-high white wood or fiber-glass boards surround the rink and support another four-foot section of safety glass.

Red and blue lines divide the ice surface into sections. Two red goal lines run across the ice ten feet from each end of the rink. In the middle of these goal lines stand the goal cages four feet high and six feet wide. Attached to two red posts and a crossbar is a white nylon net. The goal crease, or area in which the goalie operates, stands directly in front of the goal cage and is marked by a thick line. While it used to be rectangular in shape, the goal crease is now a semicircle.

Two blue lines stretch across the ice sixty feet from each goal line. They divide the rink into three sections. The defending zone for each team is the area immediately in front of its goal, where the team defends its goal cage. The neutral zone rests in the middle of the ice, and the attacking zone for each team is the area immediately in front of its opponent's goal, where a team tries to place the puck into the other team's net. Professional hockey arenas also have another red line that divides the rink in half.

Nine circles on the ice indicate places where play resumes after a halt. Referees

In the past, the goal crease was rectangular in shape.

drop the puck in the circle that is closest to where the action halted. The blue center ice spot, one foot in diameter, rests in the middle of the ice and is surrounded by a center circle fifteen feet in radius. Four other similar spots and circles, two in each end, stand near the goal area, and four additional face-off spots one foot in diameter rest inside the neutral zone.

Players' benches rest behind the sideboards in the neutral zone. Directly across the ice stands the penalty box, where a player must sit out the game for a specified period of time if he commits an infraction.

To advance the puck, players use a wooden or aluminum stick with a blade at the end. The blades may be no longer than 12.5 inches and no wider than 3 inches. Goaltenders use a different stick with a broader surface.

All players wear a shirt, knee-length pants, stockings, heavy leather gloves, skates, and a helmet. Most athletes add op-tional protective equipment, such as elbow and hip pads, and visors that shield the face and eyes. Goaltenders, because they have to block shots that approach speeds of one hundred miles per hour, wear face masks and large chest pads and use a huge glove. The puck is a hard rubber disk, weighing about six ounces, that is three inches in diameter and one inch thick.

Each team consists of a goaltender, two defenders, one center, and two forwards. The game, which today lasts for three twenty-minute periods, begins at center ice with a face-off, in which the official drops the puck and the opposing centers attempt to gain control of it.

The team with the puck then charges toward its opponent's goal. The person who gains possession may skate with the puck all the way down the ice to the other goal area or pass the puck back and forth among the players. Players may not kick the puck or advance it with their hands.

PENALTIES

Sometimes during hockey games, one team must play shorthanded, which gives their opponent a huge, if momentary, advantage. This occurs when a player is sent to the penalty box by officials for committing an infraction. For what are considered minor infractions, such as tripping or holding an opponent, a player must sit in the penalty box for two minutes; major penalties, such as injuring an opponent, bring five minutes.

Should the opponent score a goal during that two-minute span, the player may leave the penalty box.

In rare cases a referee may call a penalty shot. This happens when an attacking player is pulled down from behind as he nears the goal area. While the other eleven athletes watch from the side, the tripped player is allowed to skate in on the goalie and take one shot.

Because they often block high-speed shots, goalies must wear masks and extra padding.

Teams receive one point each time they shoot the puck past the opposing goaltender into the net. The team with the highest total at game's end is the winner. In the event of a tie, a five-minute overtime is added, and the first team to score wins the game. If the teams remain tied at the end of overtime, a tie is declared. The only exception is during the postseason playoffs, when teams continue play until one team wins.

Today's equipment and rules took years to perfect. As that transformation unfolded, professional hockey overtook the amateur version in popularity.

CHAPTER 2

"The Fastest Game in the World"

THE EARLY DECADES of the twentieth century saw rapid developments in hockey. The first professional leagues coalesced to form today's preeminent organization, the National Hockey League, while the sport spread south to the United States. New rules revolutionized the game, and owner-player relations and violence in games foreshadowed what would be major issues later in the century. After an initial expansion built the NHL to ten teams, economic woes reduced the ranks to the six teams that would carry the sport into the future.

The First Professional Leagues

Amateur hockey dominated the early years, but it was professional hockey that popularized the sport within North America. American J. L. Gibson organized the first professional league in 1904 with the International Pro Hockey League based out of Michigan. Gibson lured the best Canadian athletes, including Fred "Cyclone" Taylor, who drew enormous crowds wherever he played and earned the then-astounding salary of $500 per game.

Four years later the establishment of the Ontario Professional League led to the rapid formation of other Canadian professional leagues, including the National Hockey Association, which opened in 1910 with five teams anchored around a squad in Montreal called Les Canadiens. Wealthy businessman Ambrose O'Brien assembled one of the finest squads of those years with the Renfrew Millionaires.

Among others, the team consisted of Cyclone Taylor (who had been signed from Gibson's team) and two brothers who would later gain fame as hockey promoters, Lester and Frank Patrick.

After playing for Renfrew, the Patrick brothers headed west to develop hockey in Canada's Pacific regions. To compete with the more established leagues back east, the Patricks relied on innovative ideas for their Pacific Coast Hockey League (PCHL), such as artificial ice rinks so that the games could be held indoors and numbers on players' jerseys. They were so successful that by 1912 the PCHL champion played the eastern champion for the Stanley Cup.

For the next five years the Patricks battled eastern owners for hockey supremacy, but they suffered from the absence of big cities in the west. Without huge population centers from which to draw support, the Patricks could not long afford to pay top salaries to their stars, who soon drifted to the eastern clubs.

In 1917 the National Hockey Association became the National Hockey League (NHL). Two teams from Montreal, the Canadiens and the Wanderers, joined squads from Toronto and Ottawa to put on the NHL's first season. On December 19, 1917, the Wanderers defeated Toronto, 10–9, in front of seven hundred people, with Wanderer defenseman Dave Ritchie tallying the first goal in NHL history one minute into the game.

The league's first superstar, Joe Malone of the Montreal Canadiens, scored an amazing forty-four goals in twenty games that first 1917–1918 season, a record that would stand until 1945. The speedy Malone, who had the ability to suddenly materialize in front of the goalie like a ghost, combined modesty with his Hall of Fame talent. "I used to play practically the whole game," he said later. "We'd have two or three utilitymen on the bench, but they'd only play if someone got hurt. So I think I had more chances to score."[7]

Two other top talents were the Canadiens' Howie Morenz and, after the Boston Bruins joined the league in 1924, defenseman Eddie Shore. Morenz, called the "Stratford Streak" for his agility on skates, led his team to Stanley Cup championships twice, and both times was voted the league's most valuable player. When he died on March 8, 1937, following a serious leg injury sustained in a game, thousands of mourners lined up to walk past his coffin lying in state in Montreal's hockey arena.

SEVEN IN ONE!

One of the early superstars in hockey, Joe Malone, set a record that still has not been matched. On January 31, 1920, he scored seven goals in one game against the Toronto St. Patricks. Even though players as great as Gordie Howe, Bobby Orr, and Wayne Gretzky compiled numerous records on their own, neither they nor any other player has equaled this one by the immortal Malone.

Playing for the Montreal Canadiens, Howie Morenz was one of the early superstars of the NHL.

dangling by a thread. He ordered the physician to quickly sew him up without anesthesia so that he could return to the ice. In spite of the violence, Shore's talent brought him four Most Valuable Player Awards.

The infant NHL faced an immediate problem with World War I (1914–1918), which siphoned off many of the league's stars for overseas military duty even before the league opened for business. On November 6, 1917, one month before the league's first game, a *Toronto Globe* headline warned, "Pro Hockey on Last Legs."[8] The situation soon appeared more perilous when the Wanderers had to pull out of the league after their arena burned down. The remaining three teams, however, continued play into the '20s, when the game tapped a new source of support.

Whereas Morenz represented the flashy, deft touch, Eddie Shore typified the rough, tough bruiser. Shore abandoned finesse in favor of brute strength and rarely missed an opportunity to skate directly over an opponent. Over the course of his career, Shore amassed 978 stitches, 19 broken noses, 5 shattered jaws, and an assortment of fractures and strains. After one vicious fight, Shore went to the dressing room with his ear

Into the United States

Canadian hockey took its first steps toward becoming an international sport in 1924 when the Boston Bruins became the first American team accepted into the league. NHL promoters knew, however, that to succeed in the United States, they needed to attract the immense New York market. The following year, New York entertainment executive Tex Rickard agreed to host a hockey game at his Madison Square Garden in New York City as long as Howie Morenz played in the game. Morenz brought his Canadiens into the Garden on December 15, 1925, and, before a huge crowd of New York's financial and sporting community, scored a goal in a 3–1 victory over the New York Americans.

When the New York Americans attracted more than seventeen thousand fans to another game, Rickard was convinced that hockey could be a profitable enter-

prise, and he started his own team, the New York Rangers. The team quickly attracted a loyal following, and hockey fans at the Garden often spotted sports luminaries like baseball's Babe Ruth and Lou Gehrig among the spectators. By 1934, five other American teams began playing in the NHL, including squads from Detroit and Chicago.

The American teams played with a show business touch not seen in Canada. The New York Americans skated onto the ice

Eddie Shore of the Boston Bruins. In 1924, the Bruins became the first NHL team to operate in the United States.

for their 1925 game against Montreal brightly clad in red-white-and-blue uniforms bearing stars and stripes. Montreal player Aurel Joliat commented, "Geez, they looked like they'd come right out of a circus. We didn't know whether to play hockey against them or ask them to dance."[9]

Placing teams in New York and Boston put the NHL on sound financial footing, mainly at the expense of the Patrick brothers' PCHL. With top salaries relocating more of their stars to the United States, the Patricks closed down their league and moved east to join the thriving NHL. Lester Patrick accepted a position with the Ranger organization, where he popularized the game in the United States by explaining the sport's intricacies to New York sports reporters.

Paul Gallico, one of New York's finest sportswriters, thought he knew the answer to hockey's appeal in U.S. cities:

I have always suspected that the real appeal of hockey, and the reason for its im-

mediate success when introduced from Canada in 1925 are that it is a fast, body-contact game played by men with clubs in their hands and knives lashed to their feet, since the skates are razor-sharp, and before the evening is over it is almost a certainty that someone will be hurt and will fleck the ice with a generous contribution of gore before he is led away to be hemstitched together again.[10]

From 1926 to 1936 no one team dominated hockey; eight clubs won the Stanley Cup during those years even though most of the talent came from Canada. That gave each team time to grow and establish interest in different cities, rather than creating a league in which fans in one town were constantly humiliated by a powerhouse team from another city.

A handful of American-born players entered the league, but they faced a hostile reaction from Canadian players, who viewed them as interlopers on their national game.

YOU WANT ME TO PLAY GOAL?

Lester Patrick introduced many innovations to hockey, but his most unique contribution may have occurred in the 1928 Stanley Cup finals. The forty-four-year-old coach of the New York Rangers watched his goalie fall to the ice after being hit in the face by the puck. Since teams only carried one goalie in those days, Patrick asked opposing coach Eddie Gerard of the Montreal Maroons if he could substitute a goalie who watched in civilian clothes from the stands. Gerard declined, and jokingly suggested that Patrick suit up. Though Patrick had long ago given up his playing days, he accepted the challenge, put on a uniform, and stopped eighteen of nineteen shots, leading his team to a 2–1 overtime victory.

The New York Rangers battle the Detroit Red Wings in a 1944 contest. Despite hockey's expansion into major U.S. cities, the sport was still dominated by Canadians.

Player Aldo Palazzari said that after he joined the New York Rangers, his Canadian teammates made him feel like an outcast. Other players had to prove they could fight before their Canadian teammates accepted them.

One American athlete who stood out in those formative days was Taffy Abel from Michigan. The enormous player, who weighed 245 pounds, knocked opponents about with such ease that one family member

New Rules Bring a Faster Game

Along with its expansion into the United States, the NHL introduced a series of rules from 1918 to 1942 that drastically changed the game. Alterations had begun shortly before the league emerged. They included the introduction of three twenty-minute periods of play instead of two thirty-minute halves and lowering the number of players on the ice from seven to six in 1912. The NHL added its own wrinkles in 1918 by modifying a rule that allowed the goalie to fall to the ice to block a shot. The previous rule required the goaltender to remain standing, and even fined him $2 for each infraction, but goalies had perfected the art of "accidentally" falling down when making saves. League president Frank Calder dropped the old rule, explaining, "As far as I'm concerned, they can stand on their head if they choose to."[13]

Taffy Abel was one of the first American hockey players to stand out in the NHL.

claimed, "Off the ice, he was easygoing. On the ice, you didn't want to meet him."[11]

In 1937 the Chicago owner stunned the NHL by playing five Americans, but they skated to a dismal 6–2 loss. Observers called it "the most farcical thing ever attempted,"[12] and accurately claimed that though the NHL existed in American cities, the league relied on Canadian-bred players for its talent. This assertion underscored the fact that hockey had a long way to travel before it became an international sport.

The most revolutionary rule changes dealt with forward passing. Before 1918, players were not permitted to pass the puck forward to teammates. They had to either stickhandle—advance the puck with the stick—toward the opposing goal on their own or pass back to other players. This tended to slow the game's pace and dampen the excitement. In 1918 forward passing was allowed, but only in the neutral zone. When this made little difference, the league opened all three zones to the forward pass in 1928.

The difference was startling. The game's speed dramatically increased from the pace of an individual skater rushing up the ice to the speed of the puck being passed forward. Players had more scoring opportunities because the opposing defense could be surprised with an accurate pass, and they became more creative in skating and executing passing patterns. Athletes without the puck were now more important to a team's offense, because they could skate to an open area, receive a pass, and charge the goal.

Lester Patrick explained the value of the rule changes:

I believe in keeping the game wide open. Our followers are entitled to action, not for a few brief moments but for three full 20-minute periods a game. The open style of play calls for better stick-handling and speedier play. What better system could the coaches and managers adopt to preserve and further popularize the fastest game in the world?[14]

As a result, the game's first famous "lines" came into existence—three offensive players who joined on the ice to produce an attack. Cooperation, not individual play, became paramount. Boston's "Dynamite Line" of Cooley Weiland, Dit Clapper, and Dutch Gainor ignited the team to a 38–5–1 record in the 1929–1930 season, while the Rangers line of Bill Cook, Frank Boucher, and Bun Cook garnered Stanley Cup championships in 1928 and 1933.

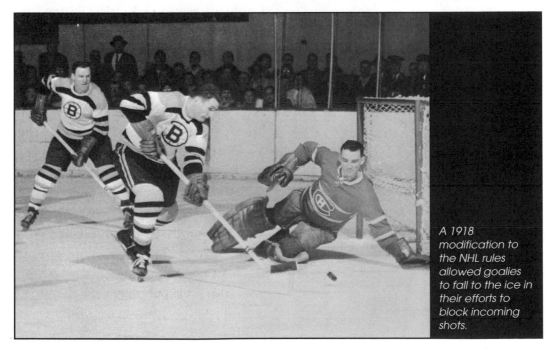

A 1918 modification to the NHL rules allowed goalies to fall to the ice in their efforts to block incoming shots.

A Taste of the Future

While the league continued to develop support and achieve profitability, a few events hinted at troubles to come. Star player Joe Malone began playing only part-time because of his poor salary, explaining that his regular job in Quebec provided a stable future that hockey could not promise. Malone's salary squabble foreshadowed player-owner conflicts that would plague the league in the coming years.

The first players' strike in NHL history created havoc during the 1925 season. A team from Hamilton captured the league title and drew a bye into the Stanley Cup playoffs while Montreal and Toronto, the second and third place teams, played for the right to face Hamilton. Now that they had reached the playoffs, the Hamilton team, upset that the number of regular-season games had been increased from twenty-four to thirty without a corresponding raise in salary, threatened to withdraw from the competition unless each athlete received $200.

Reaction from the owners was predictably swift and punitive. League president Frank Calder quickly cautioned them against such a hard-line approach, but when the players remained adamant, Calder himself declared that whichever team won the Montreal-Toronto series would take home the Stanley Cup. He then suspended the Hamilton team and fined each player $200.

Violence on the ice is a long-time problem that still plagues the NHL today.

The owners had won this battle, but it was a prelude of others to come.

Besides player-owner disputes, the NHL faced a problem that continues to the present. Violence has always been a part of Canadian hockey. A description of a 1917 game between Montreal and Seattle was typical of its day:

> Harry Mummery threw himself into Jack Walker with such force that the frail forward of the Seattle team had to be stretched out and carried off the ice. Mummery and Rickey swung their sticks on one another's heads so hard that the raps could be heard up in the [highest reaches]. Then Rickey and Couture staged a bout that would have furnished a lively reel for the movies.[15]

Part of the problem rested in the prevailing attitude throughout the league that a player had the right to fight or use rough tactics. Famous Toronto defender Francis "King" Clancy described a conversation he had with a coach in amateur hockey before he entered the NHL. The coach asked Clancy, who at five feet seven inches was much smaller than the other players, what the hockey stick was used for. Clancy replied, "Why sir, you can handle the puck with it, you can shoot with it, and you can pass."

"Very good, Clancy!" replied the coach. "What else can you do with it?"

A TWO-DAY GAME

One 1933 Stanley Cup playoff game lasted portions of two days. When the April 3 game between the Boston Bruins and Toronto Maple Leafs ended in a scoreless tie, the teams headed to sudden death overtime. After five twenty-minute overtime periods, the teams remained deadlocked. Weary after such a lengthy match, the teams asked league president Frank Calder if they could resume play the following day, but he ordered them to stay on the ice and complete the game. Finally, in the early morning hours of April 4, Ken Doraty of the Maple Leafs tallied the winning goal five minutes into the sixth overtime period.

Clancy could think of nothing else and said, "I guess that's just about all you can do with it."

"No, Frankie, it's not all you can do with it." The coach took his stick and jabbed Clancy in the ribs. "You're just a little fellow, so I want you to remember this. In order to take care of yourself when you're on the ice, this thing is always the equalizer. The hockey stick is always the equalizer."[16]

One of the most flagrant applications of violence came on December 12, 1933. Boston defenseman Eddie Shore hit Toronto player Ace Bailey from behind with such an impact that Bailey flipped in the air and crashed onto the ice head first with a sickening thud. As stadium spectators hushed, other players rushed to Bailey's aid, but found the unconscious athlete barely breathing and his legs shaking uncontrollably.

Two neurosurgeons at a local hospital worked all night to relieve the pressure on Bailey's brain. The outlook appeared so dim that local newspapers carried his obituary and the Toronto owner gave instructions on how Bailey's body was to be returned to Toronto. Bailey's father, who happened to be in Boston to watch his son play, scoured the town's bars with a gun in hand, intent on

killing Shore, but he failed to locate the Bruin star. Bailey rallied, and ten days later doctors removed him from the critical list.

However, Bailey never again played hockey. To help him with medical and other bills, the NHL staged an all-star game on Valentine's Day, 1934. With Bailey in civilian clothes and standing at center ice, each star skated out to shake Bailey's hand after being introduced to the crowd. One man, however, remained barely out of sight to the

The New York Rangers (white uniforms) and the Montreal Canadiens, two of the six teams that carried hockey into the postwar world, compete in 1954.

side. Finally, the announcer called Eddie Shore's name, and the Bruin defender skated toward Bailey. As the crowd quietly looked on, the antagonists stared at each other, then shook hands as the other players banged their sticks against the ice in a sign of approval.

Violent incidents caused newspapers to voice the need for action. Little was done to prohibit the bloodshed, though. The issue of violence in hockey would bother the game until the end of the millennium.

To the "Original Six"

In addition to brutality on the ice, economic concerns often plagued the NHL. Starting with the league's inception in 1917, the number of member teams rose and fell from year to year. Some teams faced financial hardships; others built loyal followings. Down to three teams in 1918, the NHL grew to ten in the 1930s, before the economic collapse known as the Great Depression knocked four franchises out of business.

At the beginning of the Depression, teams cut costs wherever possible. Owners decreed that no player would receive more than $7,500 annually, which represented a 10 percent cut in salaries. Some of the top stars withheld their services, but they returned to the lineup after a few games when league president Frank Calder threatened them with lengthy suspensions.

Teams in Ottawa and Pittsburgh folded shortly before the 1931–1932 season, reducing the NHL to eight teams. The residents of Montreal, one of the most avid hockey towns in Canada, tried to support both the venerable Canadiens and the Maroons, but they lacked sufficient resources. The Maroons closed down in 1938.

Seven teams survived to play in one division, but the lingering effects of the Depression, combined with the onset of World War II, were more than the New York Americans could afford. The team dissolved in the early 1940s, leaving six teams to carry the legacy of hockey into the postwar world. Those teams—the Montreal Canadiens, Toronto Maple Leafs, Detroit Red Wings, New York Rangers, Boston Bruins, and Chicago Black Hawks—affectionately called the "Original Six" by hockey advocates, constructed a firm foundation on which the 1960s expansion could take place.

CHAPTER 3

Growing Pains and Great Hockey

THE YEARS FROM 1940–1967 brought major advancements in hockey. The Original Six maintained interest in the sport despite a world war and labor strife, and the new medium of television added its potent influence to the game. While American-born players all but disappeared from the league, Gordie Howe, a Canadian athlete skating for an American-based team, re-wrote the record book. It was a time of great achievements and of growing pains.

Fierce Rivalries

The almost three decades from 1940 to the late 1960s are called the golden age of hockey, for it was during this time that the Original Six teams developed their intense rivalries and created followings in both the United States and Canada. From the turmoil of the league's formative years, in which numerous franchises collapsed and left the NHL, these six emerged as strong representatives of professional hockey. Revered teams, especially the Toronto Maple Leafs, Montreal Canadiens, and Detroit Red Wings, battled for supremacy based on the play of heroic individuals such as Montreal's Maurice "Rocket" Richard and Detroit's Gordie Howe.

Since the league comprised only six teams, few spots existed for players. From the vast Canadian pool of talent, supplemented in minuscule numbers by the largely untapped American supply, only one hundred athletes gained positions as professionals. Fierce competition not only weeded out the unskilled, but consigned numerous gifted skaters and shooters to the minor leagues, where their exploits went largely unheeded.

The men who earned places on one of the Original Six could justifiably label themselves exceptional, because they had defeated immense odds to play among the one hundred. Expansion had not yet diluted the talent; these players skated on NHL ice because their skills propelled them to the top.

With so few players inhabiting the league and with only six teams, fierce rivalries sprouted, especially between Detroit and Montreal and between Detroit and Toronto.

Each squad fought for the opportunity to claim it was the best of the best. Because teams faced each other many times in a single season, grudges carried over from game to game. A dirty hit in one contest brought sure retaliation in another. A fluke game-winning goal planted the desire for vengeance in the defeated team that simmered until the next meeting. Because the best players enjoyed long careers, the animosity continued from season to season. Consequently, these years saw numerous bench-clearing brawls and stick-swinging incidents.

Fighting also increased because the game's pace was faster than before. Rule

Maurice Richard of the Montreal Canadiens skates past Bill Gadsby of the Detroit Red Wings. Montreal and Detroit developed a fierce rivalry.

changes made it easier for swift skaters to pick up a pass and rush past defenders, who countered this new threat by slamming the skaters into the hard boards along the rink's sides, elbowing them, and grabbing them. The skaters retaliated in kind, which usually led to another fight. The intensity created devoted followings, not only in the Original Six cities but throughout all of Canada and much of the eastern and midwestern portions of the United States.

No one team dominated the league in these years. In the 1940s, for instance, Detroit won 259 games, Montreal won 256, and Toronto won 251. This balance kept excitement alive throughout the league, for spectators in any one of the six towns were sure to either be supporting a contending team or soon to be attending a game involving a contending team.

The Toronto Maple Leafs were the first of the Original Six to record an envious record. Thanks to the stellar play of goalie Walter "Turk" Broda and skater Syl Apps, who gained the nickname "Nijinsky of the Ice" for his skating prowess (Nijinsky was a famed Russian ballet dancer who lived from 1890–1950), Toronto won five Stanley Cups in the 1940s. The most impressive victory happened in 1942, when the Maple Leafs dropped the first three games of the best-of-seven series to their hated opponent the Detroit Red Wings. After their third loss, the Leafs received a letter from a Toronto schoolgirl explaining the shame she would feel if they lost the fourth game and were swept by Detroit. One of the Leafs, Sweeney Schriner, mentioned to his coach, "Don't worry about this one, Skipper. We'll win it for the little girl."[17] Amaz-

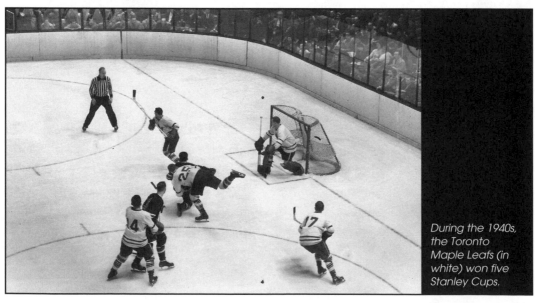

During the 1940s, the Toronto Maple Leafs (in white) won five Stanley Cups.

ingly, Toronto won the next four games to take the series and the Stanley Cup. Afterward, some of the players visited the schoolgirl to thank her for her inspiration.

Another powerhouse team, the Montreal Canadiens, behind "Rocket" Richard, goalie Jacques Plante, and Jean Beliveau, advanced to the Stanley Cup finals ten consecutive years and won it eight out of thirteen years in the 1940s and '50s. Coach Toe Blake took a squad of superstars and created a unit based on cooperation and team spirit. He also bene-

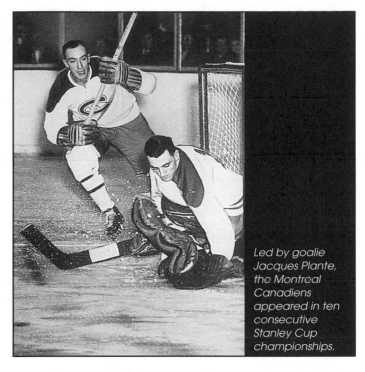

Led by goalie Jacques Plante, the Montreal Canadiens appeared in ten consecutive Stanley Cup championships.

fited from the best feeder system in hockey. Montreal controlled 750 minor league teams and 10,000 players—more than the other five teams combined—thereby ensuring a ready supply of top-notch talent.

Montreal became so successful that the league changed a rule so the Canadiens could not take advantage of it. Then as now, if a player received a penalty and had to leave the ice, the other team had a one-man advantage, called a power play, for the duration of the penalty. In those days, however, no matter how many goals the team with the advantage scored, the penalized player remained off the ice.

Montreal's power play was so imposing that they frequently tallied two or three

goals in a two-minute penalty. Finally, before the 1955–1956 season, the league changed the rule and permitted the penalized player to return to the ice after the first goal, even if time remained in his penalty.

The Detroit Red Wings, relying on the famed Production Line of Ted Lindsay, Sid Abel, and Gordie Howe and the goaltending wizardry of Terry Sawchuck, were the third team to gain multiple Stanley Cups in hockey's golden years. They won seven straight regular-season championships and four Stanley Cup titles in the 1950s. During that time Detroit fans began one of hockey's oldest traditions when a spectator tossed an octopus onto the ice during the 1952 Stanley Cup finals. The Red Wings

Gordie Howe is pictured scoring his seven hundredth goal. The second-highest scorer in NHL history, Howe led Detroit to numerous Stanley Cup championships.

had swept all eight games of the two best-of-seven series in their march to the championship, so the octopus with its eight tentacles seemed an appropriate symbol to the fan. For the next forty years fans in Detroit continued the tradition, until the NHL prohibited it in the 1990s.

A different story emerged in 1956 when the Wings faced the Maple Leafs in a semifinal match. An intense rivalry between the teams had built through the years, to the point where Red Wings player Sid Abel remarked, "They pay us to play the other teams—we'd play the Leafs for nothing."[18]

Detroit won the first two games of the series, then headed to Toronto for the next three. An anonymous caller told a Toronto newspaper, "You don't have to worry about Lindsay and Howe tonight. I'm going to shoot them." The two skaters did their best to ignore the death threat. Lindsay, who never shied from a confrontation, scored the tying goal in regulation and then the game-winning goal in overtime. After each goal he taunted the anonymous caller by inverting his hockey stick and pointing it at the hostile Toronto crowd as though he were shooting them. "If I ever wanted two or three goals in my life," he later said, "this was the night. That crackpot threat was the stupidest thing I ever heard of, but it got me mad."[19] Detroit defeated Toronto before losing to Montreal in the finals.

Three other Stanley Cup traditions date to this period. Though the custom of teams lining up after the final game of the series and shaking hands actually started earlier, it became a formal part of the Stanley Cup playoffs in the 1950s, a powerful reminder that sportsmanship goes hand-in-hand with sports. As Florida Panthers player Dave Lowry said after losing the finals to the Colorado Avalanche in 1996, "The team on the losing end of the handshakes hates like heck to do it. But it's a case of showing respect to your opponent."[20]

The other traditions allow each player on the winning team to lift the Stanley Cup and skate around the ice immediately after the final game, and gives them the opportunity to take the Stanley Cup home with them for a few days during the off-season.

They Played Their Own Game

The two players who stood out as giants in a world of imposing figures were Maurice "Rocket" Richard of Montreal and Gordie Howe of Detroit. They combined power, speed, and agility to produce records that stood for years.

The slight Richard, who stood five feet ten and weighed only 160 pounds, played with a ferocity that sometimes frightened fellow players. He loved to maneuver the puck with his stick, dash straight toward the goal, and fire such

wicked shots that goalies compared the puck's impact to cement blocks. Hall of Fame goalie Glenn Hall of the Chicago Black Hawks said, "When he [Richard] skated in on net, his eyes would shine like a pair of searchlights. It was awesome to see him coming at you."[21] Sportswriters took to calling Richard's look the "Rocket's Red Glare."

Combining power, agility, speed, and a wicked shot, Maurice Richard earned the nickname "Rocket."

HOW VALID A RECORD?

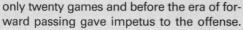

When Maurice "Rocket" Richard scored fifty goals in fifty games in the 1944–1945 season, many hockey fans placed the achievement above any other in the sport and compared it to Babe Ruth's sixty home runs in baseball. Others, though agreeing that the record established a standard for years to come, questioned its significance. Richard's scoring came during World War II, when some of the league's best defenders left the NHL to serve in the military. Joe Malone scored six less than Richard, but his came in only twenty games and before the era of forward passing gave impetus to the offense.

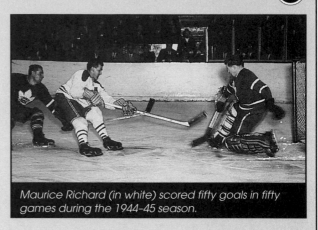

Maurice Richard (in white) scored fifty goals in fifty games during the 1944-45 season.

Whatever opinion one holds, Richard's mark has long been one of hockey's benchmarks.

His greatest feat occurred in the 1944–1945 season, when Richard tallied fifty goals in fifty games, a record that lasted for thirty-six years. His intense competitive drive, though, often landed him in trouble. On March 13, 1955, he broke a stick over the back of Boston Bruin Hal Laycoe, then smacked an official who tried to intervene. League president Clarence Campbell suspended Richard for the remainder of the season, including the playoffs.

Montreal fans did not take kindly to the suspension. Campbell received numerous death threats, and four days later a riot broke out in Montreal when he attended the Montreal-Detroit match. Montreal supporters did not calm down until the next day, when Richard broadcast an appeal for sanity.

Gordie Howe equaled Richard in every facet of the game and surpassed him in a few. He entered the league in 1946 with excellent skating and stickhandling skills, as well as a reputation for being an aggressive fighter. In his first game, Howe scored one goal and fought twice, leading his coach, Jack Adams, to bench him for fifteen games. When the punishment ended, the coach remarked, "Young man, you cannot score from the penalty box. I will not ask you to run from a fight, but please do not go looking for it." [22]

Howe survived a serious head injury in his third season, when Toronto's Ted Kennedy checked him into the boards. Brain surgery saved his life, but most teammates believed Howe's playing career had ended. The sturdy Howe returned to the ice the next season, though, and captured the league scoring title.

Richard and Howe sparkplugged the most dominant teams of their era, leading Montreal and Detroit to numerous victories and Stanley Cup championships. Richard retired following the 1959–1960 season, recording a then-record 544 total goals over the span of his career. Howe, over a remarkable twenty-six-year NHL career that ended in 1980, registered 801 goals, a mark surpassed only by Wayne Gretzky. As the sport's superstars during its golden years, the duo earned the adulation of thousands of young Canadians and Americans and the admiration of their fellow players.

Broadcast Across a Continent

Hockey received a boost in these years from radio and television broadcasts of NHL games. Radio broadcasts had started earlier, but they gained momentum in the 1940s and '50s after initial skepticism. When the first broadcast of a Montreal game aired on December 22, 1928, the local radio executive, Arthur Dupont, encountered hostility from Montreal management. He explained, "The hockey people looked upon radio with a great deal of suspicion. They feared that if stories of the games came into the

home without cost, it would ruin the attendance. So we were limited to a brief description of the third period and afterwards a summary of the entire game."[23]

Four years later, on January 1, 1933, Foster Hewitt first broadcast what would become a national institution, initially on radio and then on television: *Hockey Night in Canada.* The popular radio announcer brought hockey into Canadian homes across the land, reaching desolate areas that otherwise never would have experienced professional hockey. He also reached a newer audience in the United States, where citizens living along the border could listen

Gordie Howe's remarkable NHL career spanned twenty-six years.

to each Saturday's broadcast. Hockey legend Bobby Hull recalled that when he was young, the streets of his Ontario hometown were deserted every Saturday during hockey season because families huddled inside to listen to Hewitt's descriptions. Thousands of Canadian and American youths grew up to his voice, aping Hewitt's trademark phrase, "He shoots, he scores!"

Nineteen years later Hewitt moved to the television booth to broadcast the first televised showing of *Hockey Night in Canada*. The heated battles among the Original Six, fought by glamorous superstars like Richard and Howe, made hockey an attractive draw for television audiences. The program quickly became the most-watched show in Canada and is the longest-running program in North America. The 1999–2000 season represented the popular show's forty-seventh consecutive season.

 "MR. HOCKEY"

Wayne Gretzky may be called the "Great One," but his childhood hero enjoys the distinction of being called "Mr. Hockey." In thirty-two professional seasons spread out among five different decades, Gordie Howe scored 1,071 goals and assisted on 1,518. The gifted Howe won six scoring titles, won six Most Valuable Player Awards, and led the Detroit Red Wings to four Stanley Cup championships. His stamina even overcame a near-fatal injury. Few athletes have graced their sport with as much power and skill as the incomparable Gordie Howe.

Hoping to capture as avid an audience, American television networks purchased broadcast rights to NHL hockey. The Columbia Broadcasting System aired ten games in the 1956–1957 season and twenty-one the next year, but it failed to capture a sufficient audience to make a profit. It would be two decades before hockey achieved widespread television exposure in the United States.

Hockey Meets New Challenges

Expanding hockey to new markets through the medium of television was only one of the problems faced by the sport. As during World War I, the onset of World War II in 1939 brought changes to the game. At first, league officials considered shutting down the NHL for the duration of the war. Both the Canadian and U.S. governments intervened, however, and requested that the league continue play as a means of maintaining civilian morale.

The NHL instituted changes that reflected wartime concerns. Because of a severe rubber shortage caused by military needs, fans were asked to toss any pucks that flew into the stands back onto the ice. Officials halted regular-season overtime games because of war curfews and limited train schedules, and the renowned Boston Bruin Kraut Line of Milt Schmidt, Woody Dumart, and Bobby Bauer—all three names of German origin—dropped their label to avoid being associated with hated German leader Adolf Hitler's conquering armies. By 1943 more than eighty NHL players or coaches were serving in the military, including Toronto's Conn Smythe, who was wounded in Europe in 1944, and Dudley "Red" Garrett of the New York Rangers, who was killed in action during Atlantic escort duty in 1944.

Teams scoured wherever they could for talent to replace the missing stars. The Rangers replaced their absent goalie with one they found in an amateur Saskatchewan league. New players were brought in at younger ages, and older athletes remained beyond their productive years. These measures enabled the league to survive until its athletes returned from war in 1945.

Another change defied tradition in the name of safety. Since hockey's beginnings, players had skated without headgear. At first this posed little problem, since the puck was not lifted from the ice. But when shooters discovered that with a flick of the wrists they could veer the puck upward, concern rose over injuries to the head, especially for the goalie. Because of a reluctance to break traditions, though, not much was done for years. Since no one had ever worn protective headgear on a permanent basis, no one was about to start. Those who considered taking the first move faced being labeled by fellow players as cowardly and less manly.

Jacques Plante stood up to the criticism. After suffering two fractured cheekbones in practice, the Montreal Canadien goalie started wearing a plastic face mask. He

Jacques Plante insisted on wearing a mask for protection after being severely cut by a puck during a game.

wanted to use it during games, but his coach, Toe Blake, adamantly refused to let him wear it anywhere but in practice.

On November 1, 1959, Andy Bathgate of the New York Rangers smacked a hard backhand shot at Plante, whose view of the puck was blocked by other players. The puck tore into his cheek and nose with such force that Plante had to be helped to the dressing room, where he received seven stitches. When Blake asked if he was ready to return to the game, Plante, shaken by how closely he had just avoided major facial damage, refused to go back unless he could wear the mask. Caught without a goalie, since in those days teams carried only one goalie, Blake relented, and from that moment on Plante wore his historic mask.

WILLIE O'REE BREAKS A BARRIER

Willie O'Ree became the first black player to play in the NHL when he took the ice for the Boston Bruins against the Montreal Canadiens in 1958, but the modest individual refused to allow anyone to compare him to Jackie Robinson, baseball's first black player. He claimed that discrimination in the NHL was minimal compared to what Robinson endured in his first year and that his only thought was to be a good skater. O'Ree downplayed his own experiences, though, for he was the target of fights on the ice and slurs off of it, especially in American cities. His brief career lasted only forty-five games, but like Robinson, O'Ree had torn down one of society's barriers.

Though he still heard criticism from some players and fans that he had "chickened out," Plante refused to budge. He explained, "I already had four broken noses, two broken cheekbones, and almost 200 stitches in my head. I didn't care how the mask looked. The way things were going, I was afraid I would look just like the mask."[24]

Plante's grim determination to safeguard his body against the hard rubber puck revolutionized the game. Though it took a few more years, other goalies began to wear masks, and by the 1980s most athletes stepped on the ice with some form of protective headgear.

Even though hockey improved with the different innovations, the sport battled an image problem because of a lack of American and minority players. Before World War II a handful of Americans played in the league, but by 1960 only one existed. That total surpassed the number of black hockey players until 1958, when Willie O'Ree joined the Boston Bruins. Another thirteen years would elapse before a second black athlete skated in the NHL.

Little of substance was done until the 1990s, when the NHL joined forces with USA Hockey, an organization formed to promote hockey in the United States, to cosponsor programs for minority youth. The move produced speedy results, since by the 1998–1999 season twenty-four black athletes played in the NHL.

Other events altered the look of the league. The era of the Original Six teams ended in 1967, when the league doubled in size. The '60s, though, ushered in a new age for hockey, one that not only included different teams but introduced an international flavor.

CHAPTER 4

Challenge to Supremacy

THE ORIGINAL SIX brought stability to the NHL, but the 1960s and early 1970s changed hockey in ways the game had never seen before. A new league competed for star players and fan support, and European and Soviet hockey showed that there was more than one way to play the game. An amateur draft altered the manner in which clubs received new athletes, while a union finally united the players as a force with which the owners had to contend. To top it off, Canada and the Soviet Union engaged in a bitter eight-game exhibition that turned into a contest for hockey supremacy.

Expansion Spreads the Game

With hockey becoming more popular, it was only a matter of time before new franchises surfaced in cities that had none. The league had not expanded since the Original Six steadied the sport's decline in the

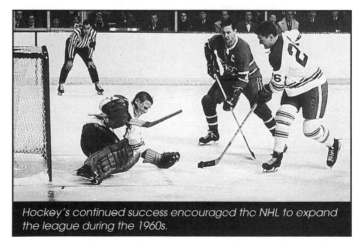

Hockey's continued success encouraged the NHL to expand the league during the 1960s.

SKILLED ON AND OFF THE ICE

Toronto Maple Leaf defenseman Tim Horton proved equally adept as a hockey player and as an astute businessman. In the 1960s he helped lead the Leafs to four Stanley Cup championships and became the team's highest-paid player. He may have contributed his most significant efforts in the commercial field, however. Before his 1974 death in an automobile accident, he built a chain of forty donut shops bearing his name. In the next quarter-century, the successful business opened more than seventeen hundred franchises in Canada and the United States.

1940s, and as the 1960s unfolded, prominent sports and business groups throughout Canada and the United States mobilized financial and civic support to bring hockey to their towns.

Another compelling reason motivating league officials to examine the possibility of expanding was the threat from a rival league. Talk circulated in the late 1960s that wealthy interests intended to open a second professional league consisting of teams in established cities, such as New York, and franchises in areas that had never had major league hockey, like Los Angeles and Houston.

To beat their competition to the punch, the NHL announced on February 9, 1966, that six new franchises would join the league for the 1967–1968 season—the St. Louis Blues, Pittsburgh Penguins, Minnesota North Stars, Los Angeles Kings, Oakland Seals, and Philadelphia Flyers. To accommodate the new teams, officials divided the NHL into two divisions of six teams each. The Eastern Division contained the Original Six, while the Western Division housed the expansion

teams. At the end of the season, teams in each division would battle in playoffs to determine the two division winners, who would then compete for the Stanley Cup. In this manner, the league guaranteed the newer franchises that one of their teams would play in the Stanley Cup finals every season.

This move doubled the number of professional teams in North America, and while the news pleased hockey fans in the United States, Canadian followers were disappointed that none of the new franchises were located in a Canadian city. To them hockey was, after all, a Canadian sport, and watching their beloved pastime head south to the United States while ignoring their native land was more than some could bear.

However, expansion delighted the talented athletes who had labored in obscurity, some for years, in Canada's minor leagues. Expansion increased the number of positions available in the NHL, and new players, eager to prove they belonged at the top level, filled the rosters. In addition, a handful of older players, who would normally have been at the end of their careers, received new life from expansion. Within seven years the NHL expanded into six additional areas. Buffalo and Vancouver joined in 1970, followed by Atlanta and the New York Islanders in 1972 and Kansas City and Washington, D.C., in 1974.

However, in its desire to build franchises in certain locations before a rival league did the same, the NHL overexpanded. A few teams experienced financial difficulties, which forced the league to take over operations. Oakland declared bankruptcy, and Los Angeles failed to attract a large following. Los Angeles owner Jack Kent Cooke, a prominent businessman who had backed other sports endeavors, had brought hockey to California because 300,000 ex-Canadians lived in the greater Los Angeles area. With dismal attendance figures plaguing his opening seasons, Cooke said with disgust, "I found out why they moved [from Canada]. They hated hockey."[25]

Overall, though, expansion proved to be a wise move, as most franchises developed avid followings in their cities. Even in the American South, where skeptics claimed hockey could never rival outdoor activities that could be enjoyed year-round, NHL teams experienced phenomenal success. In 1999 the Dallas Stars won the Stanley Cup, becoming the first team from the southern United States to be league champions.

Another step taken by the NHL was designed to develop new talent and to ensure that all teams had an equal chance at acquiring younger players. Since the league's inception, teams had constructed their own arrangements with minor league squads, which gave them the exclusive rights to all the minor league players. This system, however, favored the wealthier clubs, allowing the financially sound clubs to monopolize the talent. To remedy this, the NHL held its first amateur draft on June 5, 1963. Each team now received equal opportunity to sign fresh talent from anywhere in Canada and the United States, then assign them to minor league squads.

The draft not only helped equalize the NHL, it gradually brought an international flavor to the league. Since players were available to any team, franchises organized scouting arms to search minor league or college hockey for potential NHL players. NHL scouts studied not only Canadian talent but American high school and college-age athletes. As a sign of the future, in 1969 Tommi Salmelainen of Sweden became the first European-born player to be drafted.

The World Hockey Association Arrives

While the draft ensured equilibrium in the league, the NHL faced its first major source of competition in 1972 when the World Hockey Association (WHA) opened for play in twelve cities, six of which already featured NHL teams. The new league offered spectators fresh names, but it made its initial impact with established NHL stars.

The WHA was successful in luring superstar Bobby Hull away from the NHL.

gained instant credibility with hockey fans.

The WHA also showed more far-sightedness than its established rival by heavily scouting Europe for new talent, especially athletes from Sweden and Finland. The Winnipeg Jets in particular enjoyed success on the backs of European stars, which forced the NHL to reexamine its reluctance to mine that source.

Even with its aggressive marketing and tactics, however, the WHA struggled financially. Teams had to be moved from one city to another in hopes of luring more spectators, and some owners had trouble meeting payrolls. By 1979 the league teetered on the brink of collapse and decided to merge with the NHL. The four teams that had consistently drawn the most fans and enjoyed profitability—the Quebec Nordiques, Gordie Howe's Hartford Whalers, the Winnipeg Jets, and the Edmonton Oilers with its heralded young superstar, Wayne Gretzky—joined the NHL on June 22, 1979. Once again, one professional league served the interests of hockey fans in North America.

The WHA lured the prolific goal scorer Bobby Hull of the Chicago Black Hawks with a $2.75 million contract, and inventively persuaded former Red Wing great Gordie Howe to return to the sport with the promise to pair him on the same team as his sons Mark and Marty. The forty-five-year-old superstar, who could still skate and score against players half his age, had long mentioned his dream to one day play professional hockey with his sons. By drawing Hull and Howe into the fold, the WHA

Two Bobbys Change the Game

Fans rarely relate to behind-the-scenes maneuvering by league officials or wealthy team owners, but they are always attracted by prime-time players. In the same way that Maurice Richard and Gordie Howe dominated hockey in the 1940s and '50s, the names of two men became synonymous with hockey in the 1960s and '70s. Bobby Hull, nicknamed the "Golden Jet" because of his blond hair, powerful shot, and skating speed (almost thirty miles per hour) changed the offensive nature of hockey in the 1960s with his potent slap shot. Before Hull, players typically shot by moving the puck with their sticks and then flicking their wrists.

Depending on how hard they flicked, this maneuver succeeded in lifting the puck toward a high or low portion of the net.

Hull's shot was unique. Instead of letting the puck rest against his stick's blade, Hull lifted his stick high behind him, gathered as much strength as he could, and unleashed a potent smack that propelled the puck toward the net at speeds of up to 118 miles per hour. To gain such power, Hull bent the flat blade of his stick to create a curved blade, which caused the puck to flutter, dip, or rise unpredictably. Goalies had fits trying

Nicknamed the "Golden Jet," Bobby Hull (right) changed the nature of offensive play with his devastating slap shot.

to follow the path of Hull's shots. "You have to see it coming to really believe it," said Montreal Canadien goalie Jacques Plante of Hull's fierce slap shot. "When it hits you, it feels like a piece of lead."[26]

Hull led the league in scoring for seven different seasons. He cracked Richard's record of fifty goals in one year when he tallied fifty-four in the 1965–1966 season, and for his career he notched 610 NHL goals and 303 WHA goals.

Hull's frightening shot changed the game because players could now shoot from long-range distances. Previously, they had skated closer to the net because a wrist shot did not travel far, but now they could fire from any distance. This alteration placed more offensive strategy on power shots and less on stickhandling and passing.

While Hull changed hockey's scoring techniques, the other Bobby affected how defenders played hockey. Since the game's inception, scoring goals had been the primary responsibility of the three forward skaters. Defenders mainly stayed back to help prevent the opponent from scoring. This changed when sensation Bobby Orr entered the league in 1966. Orr, a talented defender who led charges toward the other goal, passed with a deft touch, and scored at a pace unseen for defensemen. Since he was quick enough to skate back to his defensive spot if an opponent picked up the puck, he was rarely caught out of position. Orr's exciting style of play led to a new breed of defensemen who could direct offensive charges and score as well as play defense.

The scoring ability of Bobby Orr (left) changed the way defensive positions were played in hockey.

A UNIQUE MAN

Montreal goalie Ken Dryden fit no preconceived notion of what a hockey player was like. After being drafted by the Boston Bruins during his final high school season, Dryden instead enrolled at Cornell University. He gained All-American status three times at the Ivy League school while earning his degree, then was drafted by the Montreal Canadiens. Dryden won more than three out of every four games and helped lead Montreal to six Stanley Cup championships, but despite generous contract offers from the Canadiens, he retired after only eight seasons in the NHL at the age of thirty-one.

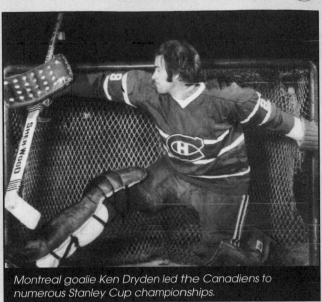

Montreal goalie Ken Dryden led the Canadiens to numerous Stanley Cup championships.

SO YOU WANT TO PLAY GOAL?

Some youngsters interested in hockey are instantly drawn to the goalie's position. Maybe it is the unusual equipment or the prospect of stopping pucks zooming forward at top speed. Hall of Fame goalie Jacques Plante points out one of the hazards of the position, however, in this excerpt taken from Brian McFarlane's *History of Hockey*:

How would you like it if you were sitting in your office and you made one little mistake? Suddenly a big red light went on and 18,000 people jumped up and started screaming at you, calling you a bum and an imbecile and throwing garbage at you. That's what it's like when you play goal in the NHL.

Goalie is probably the most challenging position in hockey.

Russian skater emerged in the NHL. However, goalie Tretiak accurately summed up the Summit Series experience: "The NHL players fired many hard slapshots, but we thought that was inefficient. We used short, quick passes to create a high percentage on net. To us, the man without the puck was most dangerous because he could go to an open area and receive a pass."[29]

Players Battle the Owners for Increased Rights

While NHL players battled Soviet stars for supremacy, they also fought team owners for improved conditions. Until the 1960s, players enjoyed few rights. Once a player signed with a club, that team held the rights to the player for life, even into retirement. Players could not withhold service or accept offers from other clubs, and when they retired they had to receive permission from their signing club if they wanted to accept a coaching position from any other organization. Players could be traded by owners or demoted to the minor leagues at will, and the minimum salary fell below $10,000 per year.

Players had discussed the idea of forming a union before the 1946–1947 season, but the talk disappeared when league owners created a retirement plan. Eleven years later Ted Lindsay of the Detroit Red Wings called a meeting among players at the annual All-

---

Few other defenders possessed the abilities exhibited by Orr. As a defender, he won two NHL scoring titles, in 1969–1970 and 1974–1975, yet captured the Norris Trophy as best defenseman eight straight years, from 1968 to 1975. Harry Howell, who earned the honor in 1967 while with the New York Rangers, foresaw what lay ahead for the league's defensemen. "I'm glad I won it now," he said, "because it's going to belong to Orr from now on."[27]

Orr scored 270 goals while leading the Bruins to two Stanley Cup championships. Knee problems forced him out of hockey after only ten years. Gordie Howe, who played more than twice as long as Orr, be-moaned the end of such a fabulous career, saying, "Losing Bobby was the biggest blow the NHL has ever suffered."[28]

Unlike other players, Orr affected the game off the ice as well. Before his time, the top rookie salary reached $8,000, but the eighteen-year-old Orr hired Toronto attorney Alan Eagleson to represent him in negotiations with the Bruins, the first time in history that the NHL had to deal with an agent. This stunned NHL owners, who had become accustomed to putting an offer on the table and waiting for the player to accept it. Now, the Bruins organization faced a hard-bargaining agent who insisted that Bobby Orr be paid what the Bruins considered an exorbitant sum of money. When Eagleson negotiated a whopping $70,000 contract for Orr in 1966, the doors opened for other players to sign agents and demand higher salaries.

In part as a result of the exciting changes in the game brought about by expansion, the WHA, and Hull and Orr, the NHL landed a profitable American television contract. With teams playing to nearly full arenas in every town, national networks decided to put hockey on the air. This helped create additional interest in the sport.

The Summit Series

Hull's and Orr's individual efforts affected the game, but hockey was also influenced by the actions of rival teams that met in the early 1970s. The WHA had taken the initial steps in bringing European players into professional hockey, but the event that most alerted the world that challengers to the NHL monopoly existed was the 1972 Summit Series between an all-star team of Canadian players from the NHL and a gifted squad from the Soviet Union. For years Soviet hockey teams dominated the Winter Olympics and World Championships, relying on pinpoint passing and complex skating patterns to confuse their opponents. Supporters boasted that they could take their elaborate style and defeat any NHL team, who relied on straight skating, hard hitting, and powerful shooting.

National Hockey League advocates responded with some truth by claiming that the Soviet Union won the amateur tournaments by illegally using professional skaters. Athletes in the Soviet Union trained year-round and received government assistance, while true amateur athletes from other countries enjoyed no such benefits. Pit actual amateur Russian skaters against the NHL, Canadians contested, and they would learn what hockey was really about.

Both nations placed their reputations on the line in 1972. The Summit Series called for eight games to be played, the first four in Canada and the remainder in the Soviet Union. Newspaper reporters designated Team Canada as the heavy favorite, even though Bobby Orr could not play because of knee injuries. When the Canadians jumped to a fast 2–0 lead in the first game, the forecasts appeared correct.

The Soviet skaters then turned on the speed and quickly erased the two-goal deficit. When the game ended with a 7–3 Soviet win, embarrassed Canadians could think of nothing to say. Some had even taken to booing their country's team. In the four games played in Canada, the Soviet team, behind star goalie Vladislav Tretiak, compiled a 2–1–1 record. The Canadian team traveled to the Soviet Union knowing that they somehow had to win three of four games to take the series, avoid humiliation, and appease their supporters, some of whom had taken to calling the rivalry a match between democracy and communism.

Conditions worsened when Canada dropped the first game in the Soviet Union, 5–4. They now had to sweep the remaining three games, which is an almost impossible task in any sport against evenly matched squads. Canada edged the Russians 3–2 and 4–3 in the next two games, setting up the final, deciding contest. Russia held a commanding 5–3 lead in the second period, but Canada came back to tie it with seven minutes left, then won the series on Paul Henderson's dramatic goal, his third ga[...] the Summit Series.

Though delighted wi[...] NHL owners and playe[...] Soviet method of hock[...] their league. NHL team[...] to Europe, especially S[...] slovakia, to sign players[...]

Since Soviet skaters [...] government from leavir[...] it would be a few more [...]

Paul Henderson (in white) struggles against Soviet players as the puck sails past Tretiak in the final game of the Summit Series.

SO YOU WANT TO PLAY GOAL?

Some youngsters interested in hockey are instantly drawn to the goalie's position. Maybe it is the unusual equipment or the prospect of stopping pucks zooming forward at top speed. Hall of Fame goalie Jacques Plante points out one of the hazards of the position, however, in this excerpt taken from Brian McFarlane's *History of Hockey:*

How would you like it if you were sitting in your office and you made one little mistake? Suddenly a big red light went on and 18,000 people jumped up and started screaming at you, calling you a bum and an imbecile and throwing garbage at you. That's what it's like when you play goal in the NHL.

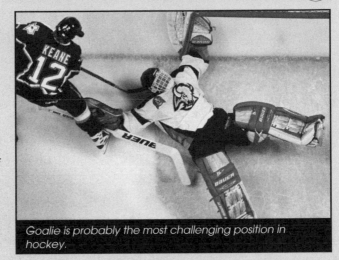

Goalie is probably the most challenging position in hockey.

Few other defenders possessed the abilities exhibited by Orr. As a defender, he won two NHL scoring titles, in 1969–1970 and 1974–1975, yet captured the Norris Trophy as best defenseman eight straight years, from 1968 to 1975. Harry Howell, who earned the honor in 1967 while with the New York Rangers, foresaw what lay ahead for the league's defensemen. "I'm glad I won it now," he said, "because it's going to belong to Orr from now on." [27]

Orr scored 270 goals while leading the Bruins to two Stanley Cup championships. Knee problems forced him out of hockey after only ten years. Gordie Howe, who played more than twice as long as Orr, be-moaned the end of such a fabulous career, saying, "Losing Bobby was the biggest blow the NHL has ever suffered." [28]

Unlike other players, Orr affected the game off the ice as well. Before his time, the top rookie salary reached $8,000, but the eighteen-year-old Orr hired Toronto attorney Alan Eagleson to represent him in negotiations with the Bruins, the first time in history that the NHL had to deal with an agent. This stunned NHL owners, who had become accustomed to putting an offer on the table and waiting for the player to accept it. Now, the Bruins organization faced a hard-bargaining agent who insisted that Bobby Orr be paid what the Bruins considered an exorbitant sum of money. When Eagleson negotiated a whopping $70,000 contract for Orr in 1966, the doors opened for other players to sign agents and demand higher salaries.

In part as a result of the exciting changes in the game brought about by expansion, the WHA, and Hull and Orr, the NHL landed a profitable American television contract. With teams playing to nearly full arenas in every town, national networks decided to put hockey on the air. This helped create additional interest in the sport.

The Summit Series

Hull's and Orr's individual efforts affected the game, but hockey was also influenced by the actions of rival teams that met in the early 1970s. The WHA had taken the initial steps in bringing European players into professional hockey, but the event that most alerted the world that challengers to the NHL monopoly existed was the 1972 Summit Series between an all-star team of Canadian players from the NHL and a gifted squad from the Soviet Union. For years Soviet hockey teams dominated the Winter Olympics and World Championships, relying on pinpoint passing and complex skating patterns to confuse their opponents. Supporters boasted that they could take their elaborate style and defeat any NHL team, who relied on straight skating, hard hitting, and powerful shooting.

National Hockey League advocates responded with some truth by claiming that the Soviet Union won the amateur tournaments by illegally using professional skaters. Athletes in the Soviet Union trained year-round and received government assistance, while true amateur athletes from other countries enjoyed no such benefits. Pit actual amateur Russian skaters against the NHL, Canadians contested, and they would learn what hockey was really about.

Both nations placed their reputations on the line in 1972. The Summit Series called for eight games to be played, the first four in Canada and the remainder in the Soviet Union. Newspaper reporters designated Team Canada as the heavy favorite, even though Bobby Orr could not play because of knee injuries. When the Canadians jumped to a fast 2–0 lead in the first game, the forecasts appeared correct.

The Soviet skaters then turned on the speed and quickly erased the two-goal deficit. When the game ended with a 7–3 Soviet win, embarrassed Canadians could think of nothing to say. Some had even taken to booing their country's team. In the four games played in Canada, the Soviet team, behind star goalie Vladislav Tretiak, compiled a 2–1–1 record. The Canadian team traveled to the Soviet Union knowing that they somehow had to win three of four games to take the series, avoid humiliation, and appease their supporters, some of whom had taken to calling the rivalry a match between democracy and communism.

Conditions worsened when Canada dropped the first game in the Soviet Union, 5–4. They now had to sweep the remaining three games, which is an almost impossible task in any sport against evenly matched squads. Canada edged the Russians 3–2 and 4–3 in the next two games, setting up the final, deciding contest. Russia held a commanding 5–3 lead in the second period, but Canada came back to tie it with seven minutes left, then won the series on Paul Henderson's dra-

matic goal, his third game-winning goal of the Summit Series.

Though delighted with the close victory, NHL owners and players admitted that the Soviet method of hockey matched that of their league. NHL teams sent more scouts to Europe, especially Sweden and Czechoslovakia, to sign players.

Since Soviet skaters were barred by their government from leaving the Soviet Union, it would be a few more years before the first

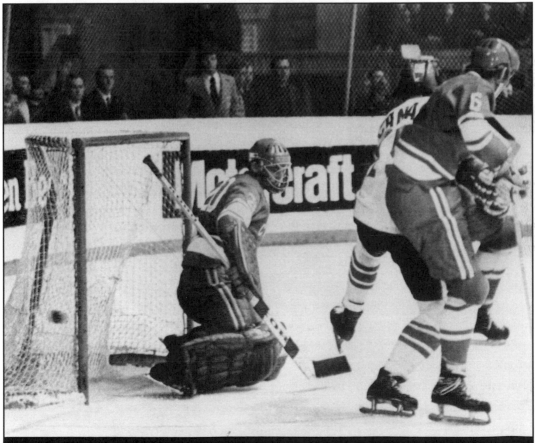

Paul Henderson (in white) struggles against Soviet players as the puck sails past goalie Vladislav Tretiak in the final game of the Summit Series.

A UNIQUE MAN

Montreal goalie Ken Dryden fit no preconceived notion of what a hockey player was like. After being drafted by the Boston Bruins during his final high school season, Dryden instead enrolled at Cornell University. He gained All-American status three times at the Ivy League school while earning his degree, then was drafted by the Montreal Canadiens. Dryden won more than three out of every four games and helped take Montreal to six Stanley Cup championships, but despite generous contract offers from the Canadiens, he retired after only eight seasons in the NHL at the age of thirty-one.

Montreal goalie Ken Dryden led the Canadiens to numerous Stanley Cup championships.

Russian skater emerged in the NHL. However, goalie Tretiak accurately summed up the Summit Series experience: "The NHL players fired many hard slapshots, but we thought that was inefficient. We used short, quick passes to create a high percentage on goal. To us, the man without the puck was the most dangerous because he could go to an open area and receive a pass."[29]

Players Battle the Owners for Increased Rights

While NHL players battled Soviet stars for supremacy, they also fought team owners for improved conditions. Until the 1960s, players enjoyed few rights. Once a player signed with a club, that team held the rights to the player for life, even into retirement. Players could not withhold service or accept offers from other clubs, and when they retired they had to receive permission from their signing club if they wanted to accept a coaching position from any other organization. Players could be traded by owners or demoted to the minor leagues at will, and the minimum salary fell below $10,000 per year.

Players had discussed the idea of forming a union before the 1946–1947 season, but the talk disappeared when league owners created a retirement plan. Eleven years later Ted Lindsay of the Detroit Red Wings called a meeting among players at the annual All-

Star Game to discuss forming a union. He argued that the owners "don't think we have minds of our own. They treat us as if we were babies."[30] The all-stars agreed to return to their clubs, conduct meetings about the issue, and collect $100 membership dues from each man.

Within four months Lindsay had the backing of every team. On February 12, 1957, he announced the formation of the NHL Players' Association (NHLPA), sparking a bitter war of words with the owners, who vowed to crush the union. By July, Lindsay and fellow Red Wing teammate Glenn Hall had been traded to the lowly Chicago Black Hawks as punishment, and Toronto benched team captain Jim Thomson, then traded him to Chicago because of his pro-union activities.

The union filed suit, trying to force the owners to grant concessions, but when the Red Wing team voted to pull out of the union in November 1957, the drive collapsed. A few months later the owners granted a few improvements to the players, such as moving expenses and better medical benefits, but true gains would not come until a strong union arrived in the 1960s.

Alan Eagleson, who had negotiated the blockbuster contract for Bobby Orr, succeeded in relaunching the NHLPA on December 28, 1966, after talks with every team. He organized the players into a solid bargaining unit that would not fold under pressure, and soon negotiated an increase in the average salary from $7,500 to $10,000 per year. For the first time, players believed they could flex their power and gain benefits from the owners.

Tumultuous times continued into the 1970s. In that decade, the long debate about violence in the sport jumped to the front pages.

CHAPTER 5

From the Broad Street Bullies to the Great One

HOCKEY ENTHUSIASTS MUST have felt as if they were riding a roller coaster during the 1970s and '80s, because diverse events bounced the sport in one direction and then another. An intimidating style of play exemplified by a team from Philadelphia known as the Broad Street Bullies became partly responsible for the league's reexamining the issue of violence. Just as the issue rose to the forefront, violence itself began to decline with the emergence of a new superstar from Brantford, Ontario, a resurgent Montreal Canadiens led by a genius coach, and increased European influence in the NHL.

Violence Plagues the League

The NHL entered an era of increased fighting and intimidation in the 1970s. Largely employing rough tactics and brute power, the Boston Bruins, called the "Big, Bad Bruins," captured two Stanley Cups in the early 1970s, followed by back-to-back championships by the even more fearsome Philadelphia Flyers in 1974 and 1975. Because of their success, other teams adopted similar strategies, and before long, fighting occupied a far more prominent place in the sport than it had before.

The Flyers garnered headlines because they were the first expansion team to win a Stanley Cup and because they were physically rough in handling opponents. The Broad Street Bullies, so labeled because the arena in which they played stood on Broad Street, accumulated penalty minutes for fighting like no previous team had before. In the 1973–1974 season, the year of their first Stanley Cup title, the Flyers received seventeen hundred penalty minutes, far more than any other squad. Writers called their arena the "cradle of licensed muggings,"[31] and league officials called for a crackdown on the violence. Flyer Dave Schultz, who amassed a league-leading 472 penalty minutes, scornfully replied, "Hockey is contact sports. It's not the ice follies."[32]

Toronto's Dave "Tiger" Williams typified players called "goons," those whose main purpose on the ice was to start fights with opponents, especially the high-scoring athletes. Williams once hit a player so hard in a fight that pieces of the player's skull entered his brain, nearly killing him. Such ruthlessness drew criticism from some quarters, but other observers simply claimed that Canadian hockey had always contained a heavy dose of violence.

The rough play was bound to have tragic results. On January 13, 1968, Ron Harris of the Oakland Seals shoved Bill Masterton of

Canadien Martin Rucinsky rakes his stick across the face of Avalanche goalie Patrick Roy. In recent years, NHL officials have attempted to curb such incidents.

the Minnesota North Stars into another player. Masterton flipped backward and cracked his head hard on the ice, causing severe brain damage. He died two days later. This incident unnerved some players. As a result, more of them began wearing protective helmets, and before the 1979–1980 season the NHL announced that any new player arriving in the league from that point on had to wear a helmet. Those already in the league would not be required to put on headgear, but they were strongly advised to do so for their own protection. Most players readily donned helmets, and the final player to skate without such a device, Craig MacTavish, retired in 1997.

Ed Jovanovski of Canada slams Ville Peltonen of Finland into the boards during a game. Hits like this may lead to fights, or cause serious injuries.

Criticism against violence mounted. Bobby Hull so detested that aspect of the game that he pulled his young son, Bobby Jr., out of the Western Hockey League because he learned nothing about the sport except how to fight. Comedians joked that spectators attended an event expecting to view a boxing match, but a hockey game broke out instead. Top executives blamed the epidemic of violence for a decline in attendance and a puny television contract.

Eventually, league officials took steps to reduce the fighting. In 1971 they announced that if a player joined a fight that had already started, he would receive a game misconduct, a penalty that included ejection from the game and a substantial fine. The NHL hoped this would prevent fights between two players from erupting into bench-clearing brawls. Five years later, in a move aimed at goons, the league assessed a similar penalty to any player who purposely started a fight.

Government authorities stepped in as well. Ontario attorney general Roy McMurtry warned that he would bring criminal charges of assault against players who used excessive violence. When Dave Williams slashed Pittsburgh's Dennis Owchar's head with his stick, requiring twenty-two stitches, McMurtry had Williams arrested. A sympathetic jury found the player not guilty, but a potent message had been delivered to the NHL.

These steps helped reduce violence and fighting, even though hockey still contains brutality. In September 2000, Boston Bruins enforcer Marty McSorley went on trial for assault with a weapon in Vancouver, British Columbia, after attacking Vancouver Canucks forward Donald Brashear with his stick. Violence in hockey may have been reduced, but fighting remains an integral part of the sport.

The Trend away from Violence Accelerates

New league rules helped diminish the problem of violence, but what carried more importance was the arrival of two teams and one individual who won championships based on skill and finesse rather than brute force. The first team to allow athleticism to overshadow brutality was the Montreal Canadiens. Coached by Scotty Bowman, a genius who would go on to win eight Stanley Cups with three different teams, the Canadiens emphasized speed, unselfishness, and passing the puck to the open man who could take a shot.

Bowman's brilliance and insistence on being in total control did not always translate into acceptance by his players, but they respected him as an individual. One of his players, Steve Shutt, claimed that team members "hated him for 364 days—and then on the other day you got your Stanley Cup ring."[33] Behind the stellar play of goalie Ken Dryden and forward Guy Lafleur, the Canadiens won four consecutive Stanley Cup titles from 1976 to 1979.

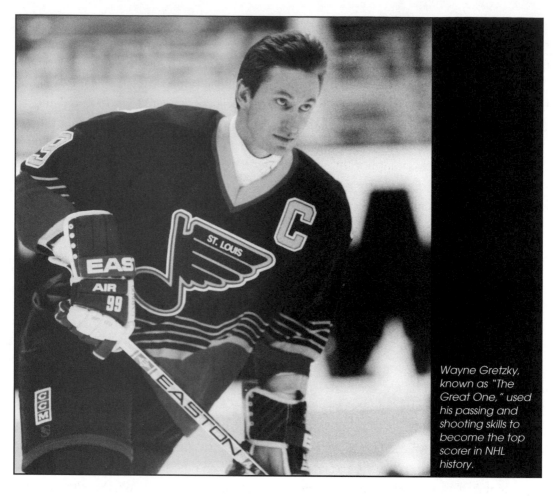

Wayne Gretzky, known as "The Great One," used his passing and shooting skills to become the top scorer in NHL history.

The New York Islanders then picked up the trend, taking four consecutive Stanley Cup championships from 1980 to 1983. Emphasizing team play and defense, the Islanders dominated the NHL in ways reminiscent of the Montreal and Detroit squads of the Original Six. They also attained their success by employing a thorough mixture of European and American-born athletes.

The major influence that shifted hockey from violence came from a young man who had made hockey headlines in grade school. Called the "Great One" since fifth grade, Wayne Gretzky's skating and scoring prowess astonished onlookers as early as his peewee league days, when spectators lined up for the youth's autograph. His accurate shooting and even better passing talents heralded a return to skill, though many observers doubted that the tiny Gretzky, who weighed barely 165 pounds, could withstand the grind of a long hockey season in the NHL.

But Gretzky perfectly fit into the Edmonton Oiler system, developed by coach Glen Sather. Sather toured Europe to visit different hockey teams, studying their practices and coaching techniques. He concluded that the elaborate passing patterns popular in Europe would succeed in Canada, so he constructed a team that mirrored that philosophy. Gretzky served as his key ingredient.

"Wayne was really the main piece of the whole puzzle," said Sather, who added that the superstar never once let down, even during practice. "He was such a great player he made the players around him better and they all developed from his confidence and the way he could play the game."[34]

Gretzky loved to stop behind the opposing goal with the puck resting against his stick, and wait for a defender to make a move. At that instant, in a barely perceptible motion, he whipped the puck across to an open teammate for a scoring opportunity. When bigger players tried to smack Gretzky into the boards, they usually hit nothing but air because the elusive skater proved so slippery.

"When he makes a pass you can't explain how he makes it," said Colin Campbell, who played briefly with Gretzky. "It flutters over, under and around things and lands on the right stick blade too many times for it to be an accident. And he masquerades his intentions so well he mesmerizes everyone on the ice."[35] Gretzky's

childhood idol, Gordie Howe, mentioned that Gretzky's style proved that hockey can be more than fighting. Instead of relying on his fists, "Wayne's the only guy who plays 70 percent of the game from the neck up."[36]

Gretzky compiled an amazing array of records. In his rookie season he led the league in scoring, he set a new scoring record the following year, and in 1981–1982 he demolished the record with ninety-two goals in eighty games. He won the league's Most Valuable Player Award nine out of ten years, from 1980 to 1989, and his 894 career goals smashed Gordie Howe's 801 as most goals in a career. Among his astounding sixty-two NHL scoring records, his feat of notching fifty goals in only thirty-nine games may be his most enduring, since fifty goals in fifty games had been the previous measure of excellence.

Former Boston Bruin executive Harry Sinden found Gretzky hard to comprehend. "Gretzky sees a picture out there that no one else sees. It's difficult to describe because I've never seen the game he's looking at."[37]

Gretzky influenced hockey off the ice when the Edmonton Oilers traded him to Los Angeles on August 9, 1988. The stunning deal shocked all of Canada, which hated to see its most famous player leave the nation, but the move helped solidify hockey's appeal in the United States. Gretzky became a big star in Los Angeles, a movie-star town already populated with celebrities, and his arrival popularized the game in California. The move led to a solid NHL television contract with American networks, including ESPN, and hastened the arrival of new franchises in other warm locales in the American South and Southwest.

Edmonton agreed to the deal because the team's owner was having financial difficulties. By trading the top star, Edmonton saved money it could use to develop younger players. Before this deal, teams traded players primarily to improve the composition of their squads, but from that point on economic considerations became a crucial part of trading.

More International, Less Canadian

The next step was to bring more international stars into the NHL. Spurred by the success of the famous Summit Series, Canada and the Soviet Union arranged additional meetings. Teams from six nations, including Canada and the Soviet Union, squared off in the Canada Cup series three times in the 1980s. The Soviet Union won the initial tournament, but Canada triumphed in the succeeding two contests to redeem its honor.

These meetings, combined with other international hockey influences brought about by the World Hockey Association and its importation of European players, lent an international flavor to Canadian hockey. In 1980 the Quebec Nordiques helped arrange the secret journey out of communist Czechoslovakia of stars Peter and Anton Stastny. Just as in a spy thriller, the brothers were smuggled out of the country and brought to Canada. This led to a new wave of European players in the NHL, including Buffalo goalie Dominik Hasek and Pittsburgh forward Jaromir Jagr, both of Czechoslovakia, and Anders Hedberg of Sweden. Similar to the way that American players had been treated upon their introduction to the NHL, some Canadian players displayed animosity to the initial influx of European stars. They believed that the Europeans took jobs that rightfully belonged to Canadians and that they played a "less manly" game that avoided hitting and fighting in favor of skating and passing.

In 1988 Sergei Priakhim opened the door for players from the Soviet Union when he joined Calgary. Within a decade, Russian skaters proved that they equally matched their Canadian counterparts. An integral part of the 1997 Stanley Cup champion Detroit Red Wings, for example, was a unit called the "Russian Five." Coach Scotty Bowman loved to confuse opponents by putting on the ice his five Russian stars, who skated rings around their competition. Sergei Federov, Viacheslav Fetisov, Vladimir Konstantinov, Vyacheslav Kozlov, and Igor Larionov dazzled fans with their intricate skating.

European skaters particularly flashed their wizardry in the 1997–1998 season, when the league's top three scorers—Jaromir Jagr, Peter Forsberg of Sweden, and Pavel Bure of Russia—all hailed from overseas. Whereas a decade earlier few players from Europe could be counted, by 1998 almost one out of four NHL athletes came from outside North America. Players on the Anaheim Mighty Ducks joked that they needed a U.N. interpreter in their locker room, where six different languages (English, French, Russian, Finnish, Swedish, and Czechoslovakian) were spoken.

Instead of being Canada's pastime, hockey now belonged to the world community of nations. At the same time, while the sport had developed and expanded mainly at the professional level and in the amateur leagues that supported the NHL, other brands had arisen that also furthered the game's interests.

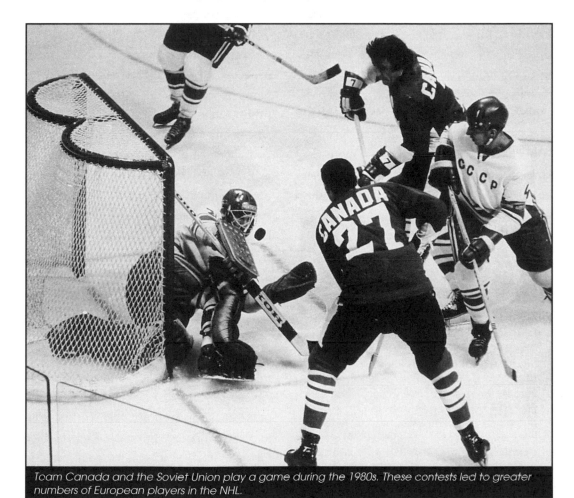

Team Canada and the Soviet Union play a game during the 1980s. These contests led to greater numbers of European players in the NHL.

International and Olympic Hockey

While Canada nurtured hockey from infancy, hockey also developed a strong following in other parts of the world. The International Ice Hockey Federation (IIHF) was formed in 1908 to govern the sport. From a beginning with five nations as founding members, the numbers have grown through the years to include most European countries. Teams from Great Britain, France, Germany, Russia, Poland, Switzerland, Sweden, Finland, and Czechoslovakia compete in various international tournaments.

International hockey always placed a premium on accurate passing and skillful skating. As such, it stood in contrast to the NHL method, which often focused more on strength and intimidation. When European stars started playing for the NHL, they influenced the way the game in Canada and the United States was played. As a result, the NHL now combines power with finesse.

Since the first IIHF World Championship in 1920, teams from Canada and Russia (formerly the Soviet Union) have taken most of the top honors. Russia has won it twenty-three times, with Canada close behind with twenty-one. The Czech Republic stands at a distant third with seven championships.

Other forms of international hockey draw support from fans. Olympic hockey has been popular for the past eighty years. Initially offering an exciting style of play by amateurs from around the world, Olympic hockey now permits professionals to compete.

Twelve nations are eligible to participate in the Winter Games. The top ten teams based on the previous year's world championships join the defending Olympic champion and a team from the host nation. The twelve are split into two groups, with each group participating in a round-robin series of five games. The top two teams in each division move on to the semifinals and play for the gold medal.

Hockey was first played in the Olympics in 1920 as part of the Summer Games in Amsterdam. In 1924 it was included as one of the cornerstone sports when the first Winter Games opened. For years Canada ruled Olympic hockey; it took the gold medal in six of the first seven Olympic Games. In that stretch, it compiled a record of thirty-seven

FETISOV AND FREEDOM

Detroit Red Wing star Viacheslav Fetisov enjoys fame and fortune now, but he did not always experience such a comfortable lifestyle. For thirteen years starting in 1975, Fetisov played for the Red Army club in the Soviet Union, the top hockey unit in the nation. Instead of enjoying the fruits of success, however, Fetisov and his teammates lived in spartan barracks near Moscow. When he peered outside, Fetisov could see fences confining him to his quarters and soldiers patrolling the area. He had little control over his life until he left the Soviet Union in 1989.

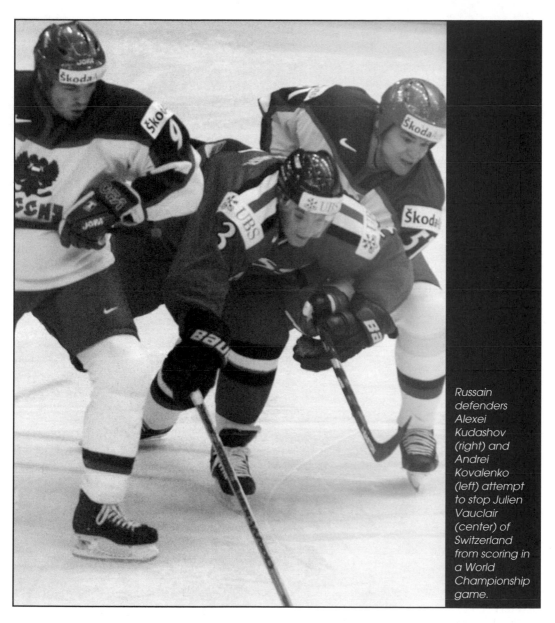

Russain defenders Alexei Kudashov (right) and Andrei Kovalenko (left) attempt to stop Julien Vauclair (center) of Switzerland from scoring in a World Championship game.

wins, one loss, and three ties and outscored its opponents 403–34.

Teams from the United States and Europe, cspccially the Soviet Union, gradually challenged that monopoly. In 1956 the So-viet Union started its era of supremacy by winning the gold medal. Other than a sur-prising defeat in 1960 to an American squad, Soviet skaters garnered every gold medal for more than two decades.

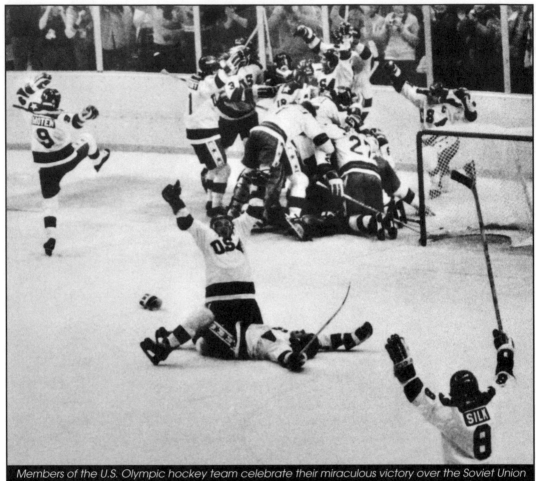

Members of the U.S. Olympic hockey team celebrate their miraculous victory over the Soviet Union in the 1980 Winter Olympics.

That came to a stunning end in 1980, again at the hands of the United States. The American team had been soundly beaten by the Soviet team, 10–3, in an exhibition game a few days before the Olympics, so no one expected much from the squad of unknowns. However, their coach, Herb Brooks from the University of Minnesota, refused to believe that the U.S. team could not play with the top

teams, and he enforced a strict training regimen, both on and off the ice to extract the best from his players.

The Americans surprised everyone by winning four of their first five games and tying the other to set up their match with the mighty Soviet team, which had won twenty-one straight Olympic games and four consecutive gold medals. Before the game, the dynamic Brooks gathered his team and reminded them that they had just as much right to be there as the Soviet team did and to simply play their own game. Brooks's words helped inspire the young squad, but they still trailed 3–2 after two periods.

In the locker room after the second period, Brooks said to his boys, "Okay, you've got plenty of time. Look at the third period as four five-minute segments. You don't have to tie it in the first one or even the second. Just stay with your system. Play your game."[38]

In the final period, the Americans skated with a vengeance, scored two goals, and held off repeated Soviet attacks to take away a 4–3 victory. A worldwide audience viewed the spectacle, labeled as the "miracle on ice." Two days later they defeated Finland to win the gold medal.

This historic game created new interest in hockey throughout the United States. Young people had new heroes in the team

AN AMAZING GOALIE

American Jim Craig proved to be one of the standouts of the dramatic 1980 Olympic hockey victory over the Soviet Union. The determined goalie stopped thirty-six of thirty-nine shots, many in the final minutes of the game when the Soviet Union threw caution to the wind in an attempt to salvage the game. Two saves, in particular, helped seal the win. With eight minutes remaining, Craig made a desperate skate save on a backhand shot by Vladimir Golikov, and with only fifty-seven seconds left, he kicked aside another shot from point-blank range.

Goalie Jim Craig is congratulated for his performance in helping the U.S. Olympic hockey team win the gold medal.

LIFE AFTER STARDOM

The twenty members of the 1980 U.S. Olympic team enjoyed varied success after their gold medal performance. Thirteen joined NHL clubs, including Jim Craig, Ken Morrow, Neal Broten, and Mike Ramsey. Broten added to his luster by playing for the Stanley Cup champion New Jersey Devils in 1985–1986, while Morrow joined the New York Islanders to become a key factor in their four consecutive Stanley Cups. Olympic team captain Mike Eruzione, however, retired immediately after the Olympics, stating that nothing he could do in sports would ever match the thrill of the 1980 victory.

members, including captain Mike Eruzione, defenseman Ken Morrow, and goalie Jim Craig. For the first time, hockey fever swept parts of the nation beyond the northern states.

The Soviet Union returned to form by winning the next two Olympic Games. In 1992, after the dissolution of the Soviet Union, the Unified Team consisting of athletes from its former nations captured yet another medal, while Sweden took the gold medal in 1994.

A monumental change occurred in the 1998 Games when professional players were allowed to participate in the Olympics. The NHL halted play for two weeks in the middle of the season to accommodate the athletes who had been selected to play for their homelands. Many NHL stars, such as Paul Kariya, Brett Hull, and Eric Lindros, traveled to Nagano, Japan, where the United States and Canada arrived as the early favorites. Surprisingly, the squad from the Czech Republic, behind the fantastic goaltending of Dominik Hasek, won the gold medal by defeating Russia in the championship game. The U.S. and Canadian teams finished out of the medal hunt.

Exciting international contests heralded new directions for hockey, which no longer was monopolized by Canada. In the 1990s, the sport expanded into other areas.

CHAPTER 6

"From a Redneck League to an International One"

Hockey entered the new millennium filled with promise. Labor turmoil of the 1990s eventually produced a harmonious relationship between management and players, and a new league president instilled modern business and marketing practices. Other forms of hockey heralded fresh variations of the game that would augment the form offered by the NHL.

Gary Bettman Takes Over

To lead the league beyond the year 2000, NHL owners looked to a man who had achieved great success organizing a competing sports world—the National Basketball Association (NBA). As its commissioner, Gary Bettman had taken the NBA to new financial heights in the 1980s by combining the star appeal of such players as Michael Jordan, Earvin "Magic" Johnson, and Isiah Thomas with clever marketing programs. Players' images graced posters, student notebooks and lunch boxes, and community service ads. Clashes between supposedly bitter foes, such as the combative Detroit Pistons with their "Bad Boys" image against the alluring Los Angeles Lakers and their majestic superstars, captured headlines. By one means or another, Bettman kept the NBA in the minds of spectators.

NHL owners viewed the NBA's accomplishment with envy. To attain similar success, on December 11, 1992, they signed Gary Bettman to be the league commissioner. Before he agreed to head the NHL, Bettman demanded that total power reside with him. Without it, he feared that any changes he wanted to make would take too much time, which is lethal in marketing a product whose success relies on speedily getting out the proper image.

Marketing executives in big-name companies warmed to the arrival of Bettman. Whereas the NHL had previously shunned most relationships with businesses, Bettman emphasized the profitability of the league's working closely with commercial firms. Bettman believed that the NHL could promote products manufactured by different businesses, such as jerseys, sticks, and pucks, while the industrial firms would pay large fees in return. Tony Ponturo, who worked in media relations for Anheuser-Busch, said the NHL had been "sort of sleepy in marketing themselves" until Bettman came along. "We got excited about the new attitude of Bettman and his people. They offered all the ingredients in the pot, with the potential for big growth for a reasonable price."[39]

Boston Bruin executive Harry Sinden praised the move. "In hindsight, he's exactly what we needed. We couldn't have had a better person at the right time, in the

Through successful marketing strategies, Commissioner Gary Bettman helped the NHL achieve new levels of popularity in the 1990s.

right place. We got someone with energy, with knowledge, a guy who is current, upscale, vibrant—and someone who wasn't locked into our stupid traditions."[40]

The NHL had previously promoted only the game's major superstar, Wayne Gretzky, while ignoring many of the other athletes. Bettman marketed all the players, and he targeted children and teens ages six to sixteen. He figured that if he hooked a new generation on hockey, when they grew up to be parents they would purchase tickets and take their children to games, just as parents had done for years past with American baseball.

Shortly before Bettman joined the league, five teams had been selected to enter the NHL—the San Jose Sharks in 1991, the Ottawa Senators and Tampa Bay Lightning in 1992, and the Florida Panthers and Anaheim Mighty Ducks in 1993. With the NHL now in five important new markets, Bettman orchestrated a profitable national television contract with Fox-TV, ESPN, and ESPN2. Later in the decade, Bettman oversaw another round of expansion, with the Nashville Predators joining the league in 1998, the Atlanta Thrashers in 1999, and the Minnesota Wild and Columbus Blue Jackets in 2000. Strengthened from Bettman's marketing expertise and solidly entrenched in most major American and Canadian population centers, the thirty-team NHL faced rosy prospects for the future.

Still, critics wondered if the NHL could ever match the money-making potentials

JOY, THEN SORROW

As tradition permitted, every member of the 1997 Stanley Cup champions, the Detroit Red Wings, hoisted the cup in the air and skated around the ice to the delirious shouts of Red Wing fans. The happiness was multiplied by the fact that this was their first championship in forty-two years. Unfortunately, Detroit team members and their fans could not long enjoy the moment; six days later, defenseman Vladimir Konstantinov and team masseur Sergei Mnatsakonov were seriously injured in an automobile accident. Though both survived, neither man has yet regained the use of his legs.

offered by baseball, football, and basketball. Some claimed that with the arrival of golf sensation Eldrick "Tiger" Woods, even golf would surpass hockey.

Others contended that Bettman committed the league to an excess of expansion that, instead of spreading professional hockey to new locales, would only bring a diluted product into major markets. Pierre Page, former coach of Anaheim, however, claimed that expansion posed no problem. "We can expand because of the Europeans. We've gone from a redneck league to an international one."[41]

A Stronger Union

Bettman was not the only business genius to benefit the NHL. While Bettman took care of league business, Robert Goodenow organized the union into an efficient instrument for gaining players' rights. On January 1, 1992, Goodenow took over for the embattled Alan Eagleson, who lost favor with many of the players for what they considered an overly friendly relationship with the owners and for his illegal use of union funds. Eagleson resigned in 1991, stood trial for embezzlement, and served time in a Canadian jail.

Goodenow acted quickly to alert the NHL that the union expected its demands to be heard. He believed that players did not have proper control over the licensing of their likenesses on items such as trading cards, nor did they enjoy a pay structure equal to their status, so in April 1992 he led a league-wide strike. He cleverly called the strike as the 1991–1992 season neared its final weeks, knowing that the owners would receive pressure from fans to settle in time for the Stanley Cup playoffs to begin.

Goodenow's ten-day strike succeeded. The players gained substantial control over where their images were used and gained a bigger share of playoff revenues. More importantly, they gained the respect of the owners, who realized that the union was serious about achieving improved conditions for its members.

Two years later a bitter union-management battle caused the NHL to close for 103 days. The players held out for improved wage and pension benefits, while the NHL claimed it had to curb the levels on spiraling salaries and costs. Before athletes reported for the season, NHL owners shut down camps and locked out the players. The settlement, which came almost four months later, gave players the right to move from team to team, while granting to owners the right to impose a limit on salaries. Forty-eight games were salvaged for the 1994–1995 season.

Women's Hockey Comes to the Fore

Male hockey players fought for additional benefits; female hockey players battled for recognition and acceptance. Most spectators assume that women's hockey is a newcomer to the scene, but the first recorded instance of a women's contest occurred in 1886, when Annie McIntyre organized a women's hockey team in the Canadian province of Saskatchewan. Three years later Isobel Stanley, the daughter of Lord Stanley who donated hockey's famous trophy, joined other women on a government team to compete against another female team. By the early 1900s, women's hockey clubs flourished throughout Canada. Calgary, Toronto, Montreal, Ottawa, and Quebec were among the large cities featuring women's teams.

Women continued to play hockey into the 1940s. The most outstanding unit of those days emerged from Ontario, where the Preston Rivulettes lost only two times in more than 350 contests. From 1930 to 1940, the Rivulettes reigned as the Canadian women's hockey champions.

The sport experienced a decline in the 1940s and '50s. Since World War II (1939–1945) took so many men out of the workforce and placed them into the military, women were needed to fill the open jobs. Instead of picking up a hockey stick, women athletes lifted hammers and power drills and headed to factories. When the war ended and the men returned, society frowned on independent-thinking women. The place for a woman, the prevailing attitude contended, was in the home, not at the hockey rink.

One exception stood out. In 1956 nine-year-old Abby Hoffman was selected to play in a hockey tournament because of her outstanding season. All season long Abby had dressed for games at home and wore her hair in a short, boyish style, enabling her to mask the fact that she was not a boy. Only when tournament officials examined her birth certificate, which was then a requirement, did they learn that Abby was a girl, and they subsequently banned her from playing.

Abby's family took legal action, but the Ontario Supreme Court upheld the ban. Abby could no longer play hockey (although she later competed in four Olympic Games as a track and field athlete), and

WHAT MIGHT HAVE BEEN

Wayne Gretzky and Gordie Howe share most of the scoring records in the NHL, but Mario Lemieux of the Pittsburgh Penguins might have topped them had he not endured injuries and illness. After scoring seventy goals in the 1987–1988 season and eighty-five the next year, Lemieux suffered a herniated disc. Surgery forced him to miss twenty–one games in the 1989–1990 season and fifty more in 1990–1991.

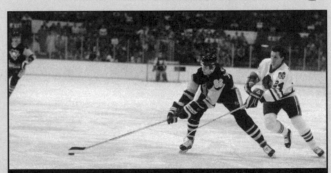

Many feel that had he remained healthy, Mario Lemieux (left) could have surpassed the records set by Wayne Gretzky and Gordie Howe.

Two years later Lemieux received worse news when doctors informed him he had Hodgkin's disease, a form of cancer. Lemieux missed another twenty games, but still came back to grab that season's scoring title. Lemieux missed most of the 1993–1994 season and the entire 1994–1995 season because of his cancer treatment. He returned to play for two more years, then retired in 1997.

Lemieux scored 613 goals in 745 NHL games. Many believe that had he been healthy throughout his career, Lemieux's records would have surpassed those of both Gretzky and Howe.

Sara Decosta, a member of the U.S. women's Olympic hockey team. Today, women have the opportunity to play hockey at all levels.

Still, the women suffered from a lack of respect. A reporter for the *Toronto Daily Star* wrote of one game, "It was a gentlemanly —oops—ladylike game of hockey with the girls, some wearing no more protective equipment than flimsy blouses, doing everything they could to keep from bumping into each other."[42]

Maria Dennis, who played hockey at Yale, recalled her constant fight to gain credibility in a sport that wished to deny it to her and other women. "Growing up playing mostly with the boys in youth hockey programs, people would come up to me and say, 'You skate so wonderfully,' and I would say, 'Thank you.' Then they'd say, 'You skate like a guy,' to which I'd reply, 'I don't skate like a guy; I skate like a hockey player.'"[43]

young girls who wanted to participate in the sport had to continue to use deception to join boys' hockey leagues.

Women's hockey enjoyed a rebirth in the 1960s and '70s, especially in the Canadian provinces of British Columbia and Ontario. Girls' teams from those areas even traveled to Japan and Finland for exhibition games. Women's hockey received such an enthusiastic reception in Ontario that by 1982 more than ten thousand girls played hockey in that province alone.

The sport did not enjoy great popularity until the 1980s, when college and high school athletic programs in the United States promoted female participation in most major sports. In 1994 Minnesota became the first state to approve women's high school hockey, while colleges across the United States, spurred by the government's requirements for equal opportunities in sports, offered women's teams. These efforts created significant interest in the sport, and the number of female hockey players in the United States quadrupled between 1990 and 1996 to twenty thousand women on seven hundred teams.

It was simply a matter of time before a female would participate in the professional ranks. That happened in 1992, although with a bit of showmanship involved. Goaltender Manon Rheaume became the first woman to try out for an NHL club when the Tampa Bay Lightning invited her to preseason camp. Manager Phil Esposito, a Hall of Fame hockey star, admitted he asked Rheaume to come for the publicity value. "I'd be lying to you if I said I didn't do this to get my team some publicity," he told the press. "I'm telling you, I'd put skates on a horse and put that out there if I knew it could stop the puck."[44]

Rheaume understood the nature of the offer, but believed she could help women's hockey by being the first female in the NHL and at least symbolically breaking that barrier. On September 23, 1992, she played the first period as goalie in an exhibition game against the St. Louis Blues, leaving with the score knotted 2–2. Three months later she made her professional debut during a regular-season game when she played goal for the International Hockey League's Salt Lake Golden Eagles. Rheaume stopped three of four shots during her six minutes of playing time. In 1998, Rheaume was named to the Canadian women's hockey squad.

Women's hockey first emerged in Olympic competition in 1998. The U.S. team, buttressed by strong college and high school programs that produced skilled athletes, was optimistic about its chances for a gold medal, even though Canada, Finland, and China received most of the media attention.

The women realized they had a chance to make an impact on their sport and become role models to young girls in their country. Coach Ben Smith mentioned that "They can already see their faces on the Wheaties boxes. They know what happened to the softball and soccer teams [both gained enormous publicity following their triumphs in earlier Olympic Games] when they won gold and that's what they want, too. This is the chance for this sport to really blossom."[45]

Smith loved working with the women, in part because he knew they had experienced such a difficult time playing hockey at high levels. "They would get chased off the rinks, but they would tuck their hair up in their helmets and come back the next Saturday for a game," Smith explained. "They were not getting paid and they didn't think there was a pot of gold somewhere. They came because they love playing. That really distinguishes them and unites them and bonds them."[46]

Led by captain Cammi Granato, the U.S. women's team upset predictions and won the 1998 gold medal by defeating Canada, 3–1. Granato, the younger sister of NHL player Tony Granato, typified how far women had come in the sport. When she was in grade school she participated in an all-boys bantam tournament dressed like a boy and registered as Carl Granato. Within a decade, she captained the female's gold medal team. "I've stayed close with my brother, and I've tried to take his work ethic," explained Granato. "He's a leader and a team player. He's taught me a lot and I listen to advice from him more than I would anyone else."[47]

Because of the American women's success, female hockey gained more devotees as the millennium approached. Granato acknowledged, "The weirdest thing is that what I was doing was so wrong in everybody's eyes when I was growing up. Now people commend you and are very excited and accepting. It's cool now for girls to play hockey."[48]

Besides the Olympics, women's hockey is featured in other international events. Since 1990, the International Ice Hockey Federation has sponsored a Women's World Championships every other year. It places the top five European teams in a round-robin tournament along with Canada, the United States, and the top Asian team. In addition, a Women's European Champi-

Sarah Teuting, goalie for the U.S. women's Olympic hockey team, defends the goal against the Canadian team during the gold medal game of the 1998 Winter Olympics.

The popularity of ice hockey has fueled the growth of in-line hockey.

onship is held every two years, and an annual Women's Pacific Championship began in 1995 to bring together Canada, the United States, China, and Japan. These examples show the extent to which hockey has diversified since its inception in Canada in the previous century.

In-Line Hockey

A more recent form of hockey combines the speed of ice hockey with the burgeoning popularity of in-line roller skating. In-line hockey, so called because the wheels of the skates align in a single row, started in California in the 1980s and quickly spread to other parts of the nation. There are currently teams throughout the world that compete in both the World Championships and the Pan-American Games, which brings together athletes from North and South America. Supervision of the fast-growing sport is handled by the National In-Line Hockey Association and by USA Hockey.

Some authorities claim that an Englishman, Joseph Merlin, invented the first in-line skate in 1760 when he attached wooden wheels to leather shoes. However, modern in-line skates were created in 1980 by Scott and Brennan Olson of Minneapolis, Minnesota. Avid hockey players, the brothers missed their favorite sport during the summer months. The two removed the blades from their hockey skates and replaced them with plastic wheels. When their new device was a hit with friends, the brothers formed their own company, started selling skates, and gave rise to a new form of hockey.

A professional league debuted in 1993 and, supported by a well-paying television

YOU TRADED WHO?

Proving that no athlete is safe in sports, the Edmonton Oilers traded their superstar, Wayne Gretzky, to the Los Angeles Kings within hours after he had helped the team win its fourth Stanley Cup. As related in the book *Ultimate Hockey* by Glenn Weir, Jeff Chapman, and Travis Weir, the stunned Gretzky explained, "I couldn't believe it. The team wanted to trade me? The team that just two hours before I'd helped to win its fourth Stanley Cup in the last five years? The team that was still young enough to win another three or four in a row? The team I supposed I'd retire with? Amazing how fast you can lose your appetite."

Wayne Gretzky celebrates after helping the Edmonton Oilers win the Stanley Cup.

contract, expanded to twenty-four teams. The game is similar to the one played in the NHL, but in-line teams use only five players on the rink—two forwards, who are usually the teams' best scorers and passers, two defenders, and a goalie. The equipment is basically the same, but the rinks consist of either asphalt, concrete, wood, or tiles instead of ice. The hard rubber puck of the NHL is replaced with a lighter plastic puck.

In-line hockey continues to gain followers for its excitement and fine play. Younger athletes play in city leagues, while skilled skaters participate in serious contests at the professional level. Bryan Trottier, who helped lead the New York Islanders to four Stanley Cup titles from 1980 to 1983, played professional in-line hockey for the Pittsburgh Phantoms after his NHL career ended.

To the Future

The rapid spread of women's hockey, international competition, and in-line skating, along with the prosperity enjoyed by the NHL, shows that the game of hockey is in superb shape as the twenty-first century opens. The professional game weathered owner-player strife, two world wars, a depression, and government crackdowns on violence to emerge stable and strong.

NHL marketing and extensive television coverage have raised awareness of the game. Hockey stars gain adulation in much the same fashion as baseball heroes or football legends, and one of the hottest items in sports apparel is a hockey jersey bearing the name of an NHL player. Success at the professional level bred greater success in youth hockey. At some locations around the nation, getting ice time for practice is so difficult that junior high school–age students wake up in the winter's early hours to attend 6:00 A.M. practice sessions, then head to school.

Fan support has risen in the league not only in Canada and the United States but also in Europe, from where a proportion- ately greater number of skaters come than before. A league that had once been the private domain of Canada has successfully embraced the rest of the world and transformed itself into an international game.

In 1997, three members of the Stanley Cup champion Detroit Red Wings took the trophy back to their homeland so that Russian citizens could gain a glimpse of the famous cup. Viacheslav Fetisov, Igor Larionov, and Vyacheslav Kozlov paraded the cup before sixty-two thousand fans in one arena. One Russian youth, twelve-year-old Dmitri Vorovjev, typified the impact that hockey holds over a younger generation:

> I always dreamt about seeing them [the three Red Wings], but I never thought I would see them live, with the Stanley Cup. I was so nervous, I was going crazy. I will go over there [to North America] some day and win the Cup myself.[49]

Awards and Statistics

Individual Records (Season)

Most Goals

Goals	Player	Team	Season (G)
92	Wayne Gretzky	Edmonton Oilers	1981–82 (80)
87	Wayne Gretzky	Edmonton Oilers	1983–84 (80)
86	Brett Hull	St. Louis Blues	1990–91 (80)
85	Mario Lemieux	Pittsburgh Penguins	1988–89 (80)
76	Phil Esposito	Boston Bruins	1970–71 (78)
76	Alex Mogilny	Buffalo Sabres	1992–93 (84)
76	Teemu Selanne	Winnipeg Jets	1992–93 (84)

Most Assists

Assists	Player	Team	Season (G)
163	Wayne Gretzky	Edmonton Oilers	1985–86 (80)
135	Wayne Gretzky	Edmonton Oilers	1984–85 (80)
125	Wayne Gretzky	Edmonton Oilers	1982–83 (80)
122	Wayne Gretzky	Los Angeles Kings	1990–91 (80)
121	Wayne Gretzky	Edmonton Oilers	1986–87 (80)

Most Points

Points (G/A)	Player	Team	Season (G)
215 (52/163)	Wayne Gretzky	Edmonton Oilers	1985–86 (80)
212 (92/120)	Wayne Gretzky	Edmonton Oilers	1981–82 (80)
208 (73/135)	Wayne Gretzky	Edmonton Oilers	1984–85 (80)
205 (87/118)	Wayne Gretzky	Edmonton Oilers	1983–84 (80)
199 (85/114)	Mario Lemieux	Pittsburgh Penguins	1988–89 (80)

Penalties

Penalty Minutes	Player	Team	Season
472	Dave Schultz	Philadelphia Flyers	1974–75
409	Paul Baxter	Pittsburgh Penguins	1981–82
408	Mike Peluso	Chicago Black Hawks	1991–92
405	Dave Schultz	Philadelphia Flyers	1977-78

Goaltender Records

Victories	Goalie	Team	Season
47	Bernie Parent	Philadelphia Flyers	1973–74
44	Bernie Parent	Philadelphia Flyers	1974–75

Victories	Goalie	Team	Season
44	Terry Sawchuk	Detroit Red Wings	1950–51
44	Terry Sawchuk	Detroit Red Wings	1951–52

Shutouts	Goalie	Team	Season
22	George Hainsworth	Montreal Canadiens	1928–29
15	Alex Connell	Ottawa Senators	1925–26
15	Alex Connell	Ottawa Senators	1927–28
15	Hal Winkler	Boston Bruins	1927–28
15	Tony Esposito	Chicago Black Hawks	1969–70

Individual Records

Most Seasons: Gordie Howe, 1946–47 through 1970–71 (Detroit) and 1979–80 (Hartford), 26 seasons
Most Games: Gordie Howe, 1,767
Most Goals One Game: 7, Joe Malone, Quebec Bulldogs, 1920
Most Goals by a Defeseman, Season: 48, Paul Coffey, Edmonton Oilers, 1985–86
Most Goals by Rookie: 76, Teemu Selanne, Winnipeg Jets, 1992–93
Most Assists by a Rookie: 70, Peter Stastny, Quebec Nordiques, 1980–81, and Joe Juneau, Boston Bruins, 1992–93
Most Points by a Rookie: 132, Teemu Selanne, Winnipeg Jets, 1992–93
Most 50 Goal Seasons: 9, Mike Bossy and Wayne Gretzky
Most 100 Point Seasons: 13, Wayne Gretzky
Most Three or More Goal Games, Career: 50, Wayne Gretzky

Career Leaders

Goals

894	Wayne Gretzky, 20 seasons
801	Gordie Howe, 26 seasons
731	Marcel Dionne, 18 seasons
717	Phil Esposito, 18 seasons
708	Mike Gartner, 19 seasons
613	Mario Lemieux, 12 seasons
610	Bobby Hull, 16 seasons
610	Mark Messier, 20 seasons
608	Dino Ciccarelli, 19 seasons
601	Jari Kurri, 17 seasons

Assists

1,963	Wayne Gretzky, 20 seasons
1,102	Paul Coffey, 19 seasons
1,083	Ray Bourque, 20 seasons
1,050	Mark Messier, 20 seasons
1,049	Gordie Howe, 26 seasons
1,040	Marcel Dionne, 18 seasons
1,037	Ron Francis, 18 seasons
926	Stan Mikita, 22 seasons

Assists

901	Bryan Trottier, 18 seasons
891	Dale Hawerchuk, 16 seasons

Points

2,857	Wayne Gretzky, 20 seasons
1,850	Gordie Howe, 26 seasons
1,771	Marcel Dionne, 18 seasons
1,660	Mark Messier, 20 seasons
1,590	Phil Esposito, 18 seasons
1,494	Mario Lemieux, 12 seasons
1,487	Paul Coffey, 19 seasons
1,486	Ron Francis, 18 seasons
1,483	Steve Yzerman, 16 seasons
1,467	Stan Mikita, 22 seasons

Shutouts

103	Terry Sawchuk
94	George Hainsworth
84	Glenn Hall
82	Jacques Plante
81	Tiny Thompson
81	Alex Connell
76	Tony Esposito
73	Lorne Chabot
71	Harry Lumley
66	Roy Worters

Goaltender Victories

447	Terry Sawchuk, 21 seasons
434	Jacques Plante, 18 seasons
423	Tony Esposito, 16 seasons
407	Glenn Hall, 18 seasons
405	Patrick Roy, 14 seasons
392	Grant Fuhr, 17 seasons

NHL Leading Scorers

Season	Name, Team	Goals	Ass	P
1998–99	Jaromir Jagr, Pittsburgh	44	83	127
	Teemu Selanne, Anaheim	47	60	107
1997–98	Jaromir Jagr, Pittsburgh	35	67	102
	Peter Forsberg, Colorado	25	66	91
1996–97	Mario Lemieux, Pittsburgh	50	72	122
	Teemu Selanne, Anaheim	51	58	109
1995–96	Mario Lemieux, Pittsburgh	69	92	161
	Jaromir Jagr, Pittsburgh	62	87	149

Season	Name, Team	Goals	Ass	P
1994–95	Jaromir Jagr, Pittsburgh	32	38	70
	Eric Lindros, Philadelphia	29	41	70
1993–94	Wayne Gretzky, LA	38	92	130
	Sergei Fedorov, Detroit	56	64	120
1992–93	Mario Lemieux, Pittsburgh	69	91	160
	Pat LaFontaine, Buffalo	53	95	148
1991–92	Mario Lemieux, Pittsburgh	44	87	131
	Kevin Stevens, Pittsburgh	54	69	123
1990–91	Wayne Gretzky, LA	41	122	163
	Brett Hull, St. Louis	86	45	131
1989–90	Wayne Gretzky, LA	40	102	142
	Mark Messier, Edmonton	45	84	129
1988–89	Mario Lemieux, Pittsburgh	85	114	199
	Wayne Gretzky, LA	54	114	168
1987–88	Mario Lemieux, Pittsburgh	70	98	168
	Wayne Gretzky, Edmonton	40	109	149
1986–87	Wayne Gretzky, Edmonton	62	121	183
	Jari Kurri, Edmonton	54	54	108
1985–86	Wayne Gretzky, Edmonton	52	163	215
	Mario Lemiex, Pittsburgh	48	93	141
1984–85	Wayne Gretzky, Edmonton	73	135	208
	Jari Kurri, Edmonton	71	64	135
1983–84	Wayne Gretzky, Edmonton	87	118	205
	Paul Coffey, Edmonton	40	86	126
1982–83	Wayne Gretzky, Edmonton	71	125	196
	Peter Stastny, Quebec	47	77	124
1981–82	Wayne Gretzky, Edmonton	92	120	212
	Mike Bossy, NYI	64	83	147
1980–81	Wayne Gretzky, Edmonton	55	109	164
	Marcel Dionne, LA	58	77	135
1979–80	Marcel Dionne, LA	53	84	137
	Wayne Gretzky, Edmonton	51	86	137
1978–79	Bryan Trottier, NYI	47	87	134
	Marcel Dionne, LA	59	71	130
1977–78	Guy Lafleur, Montreal	60	72	132
	Bryan Trottier, NYI	46	77	123
1976–77	Guy Lafleur, Montreal	56	80	136
	Marcel Dionne, LA	53	69	122
1975–76	Guy Lafleur, Montreal	56	69	125
	Bobby Clarke, Philadelphia	30	89	119
1974–75	Bobby Orr, Boston	46	89	133
	Phil Esposito, Boston	61	66	127
1973–74	Phil Esposito, Boston	68	77	145
	Bobby Orr, Boston	32	90	122
1972–73	Phil Esposito, Boston	55	75	130
	Bobby Clarke, Philadelphia	37	67	104
1971–72	Phil Esposito, Boston	66	67	133
	Bobby Orr, Boston	37	80	117
1970–71	Phil Esposito, Boston	76	76	152
	Bobby Orr, Boston	37	102	139
1969–70	Bobby Orr, Boston	33	87	120
	Phil Esposito, Boston	43	56	99
1968–69	Phil Esposito, Boston	49	77	126
	Bobby Hull, Chicago	58	49	107

Season	Name, Team	Goals	Ass	P
1967–68	Stan Mikita, Chicago	40	47	87
	Phil Esposito, Boston	35	49	84
1966–67	Stan Mikita, Chicago	35	62	97
	Bobby Hull, Chicago	52	28	80
1965–66	Bobby Hull, Chicago	54	43	97
	Stan Mikita, Chicago	30	48	78
1964–65	Stan Mikita, Chicago	28	59	87
	Norm Ullman, Detroit	42	41	83
1963–64	Stan Mikita, Chicago	39	50	89
	Bobby Hull, Chicago	43	44	87
1962–63	Gordie Howe, Detroit	38	48	86
	Andy Bathgate, NYR	35	46	81
1961–62	Bobby Hull, Chicago	50	34	84
	Andy Bathgate, NYR	28	56	84
1960–61	Bernie Geoffrion, Montreal	50	45	95
	Jean Beliveau, Montreal	32	58	90
1959–60	Bobby Hull, Chicago	39	42	81
	Bronco Horvath, Boston	39	41	80
1958–59	Dickie Moore, Montreal	41	55	96
	Jean Beliveau, Montreal	45	46	91
1957–58	Dickie Moore, Montreal	36	48	84
	Henri Richard, Montreal	28	52	80
1956–57	Gordie Howe, Detroit	44	45	89
	Ted Lindsay, Detroit	30	55	85
1955–56	Jean Beliveau, Montreal	47	41	88
	Gordie Howe, Detroit	38	41	79
1954–55	Bernie Geoffrion, Montreal	38	37	75
	Maurice Richard, Montreal	38	36	74
1953–54	Gordie Howe, Detroit	33	48	81
	Maurice Richard, Montreal	37	30	67
1952–53	Gordie Howe, Detroit	49	46	95
	Ted Lindsay, Detroit	32	39	71
1951–52	Gordie Howe, Detroit	47	39	86
	Ted Lindsay, Detroit	30	39	69
1950–51	Gordie Howe, Detroit	43	43	86
	Maurice Richard, Montreal	42	24	66
1949–50	Ted Lindsay, Detroit	23	55	78
	Sid Abel, Detroit	34	35	69
1948–49	Roy Conacher, Chicago	26	42	68
	Doug Bentley, Chicago	23	43	66
1947–48	Elmer Lach, Montreal	30	31	61
	Buddy O'Connor, NYR	24	36	60
1946–47	Max Bently, Chicago	29	43	72
	Maurice Richard, Montreal	45	26	71
1945–46	Max Bently, Chicago	31	30	61
	Gaye Stewart, Toronto	37	15	52
1944–45	Elmer Lach, Montreal	26	54	80
	Maurice Richard, Montreal	50	23	73
1943–44	Herb Cain, Boston	36	46	82
	Doug Bently, Chicago	38	39	77
1942–43	Doug Bently, Chicago	33	40	73
	Bill Cowley, Boston	27	45	72
1941–42	Bryan Hextall, NYR	24	32	56
	Lynn Patrick, NYR	32	22	54

Season	Name, Team	Goals	Ass	P
1940–41	Bill Cowley, Boston	17	45	62
	Bryan Hextall, NYR	26	18	44
1939–40	Milt Schmidt, Boston	22	30	52
	Woody Dumart, Boston	22	21	43
1938–39	Toe Blake, Montreal	24	23	47
	Sweeney Schriner, NYA	13	31	44
1937–38	Gordie Drillon, Toronto	26	26	52
	Syl Apps, Toronto	21	29	50
1936–37	Sweeney Schriner, NYA	21	25	46
	Syl Apps, Toronto	16	29	45
1935–36	Sweeney Schriner, NYA	19	26	45
	Marty Barry, Detroit	21	19	40
1934–35	Charlie Conacher, Toronto	36	21	57
	Syd Howe, St. L/Det	22	25	47
1933–34	Charlie Conacher, Toronto	32	20	52
	Joe Primeau, Toronto	14	32	46
1932–33	Bill Cook, NYR	28	22	50
	Busher Jackson, Toronto	27	17	44
1931–32	Busher Jackson, Toronto	28	25	53
	Joe Primeau, Toronto	13	37	50
1930–31	Howie Morenz, Montreal (C)	28	23	51
	Ebbie Goodfellow, Detroit	25	23	48
1929–30	Cooney Weiland, Boston	43	30	73
	Frank Boucher, NYR	26	36	62
1928–29	Ace Bailey, Toronto	22	10	32
	Nels Stewart, Montreal (M)	21	8	29
1927–28	Howie Morenz, Montreal (C)	33	18	51
	Aurel Joliat, Montreal (C)	28	11	39
1926–27	Bill Cook, NYR	33	4	37
	Dick Irvin, Chicago	18	18	36
1925–26	Nels Stewart, Montreal (M)	34	8	42
	Cy Denneny, Ottawa	24	12	36
1924–25	Babe Dye, Toronto	38	6	44
	Cy Denneny, Ottawa	27	15	42
1923–24	Cy Denneny, Ottawa	22	1	23
	Billy Boucher, Montreal	16	6	22
1922–23	Babe Dye, Toronto	26	11	37
	Cy Denneny, Ottawa	21	10	31
1921–22	Punch Broadbent, Ottawa	32	14	46
	Cy Denneny, Ottawa	27	12	39
1920–21	Newsy Lalonde, Montreal	32	11	43
	Babe Dye, Ham./Tor.	35	5	40
1919–20	Joe Malone, Quebec	39	10	49
	Newsy Lalonde, Montreal	37	9	46
1918–19	Newsy Lalonde, Montreal	23	10	33
	Odie Cleghorn, Montreal	21	6	27
1917–18	Joe Malone, Montreal	44	4	48
	Cy Denneny, Ottawa	36	10	46

Playoff Record Holders

Goals

Career: Wayne Gretzky, 122; Mark Messier, 109; Jari Kurri, 106

Season: Reggie Leach, Philadelphia, 1976, 19; Jari Kurri, Edmonton, 1985, 19; Joe Sakic, Colorado, 1996, 18

Series other than final: Jari Kurri, Edmonton, 1985 Conference Final, 12

Final Series: Babe Dye, Toronto, 1922, 9 in 5 games

Game: Newsy Lalonde, Montreal, 1919, 5; Maurice Richard, Montreal, 1944, 5; Darryl Sittler, Toronto, 1976, 5; Reggie Leach, Philadelphia, 1976, 5; Mario Lemieux, Pittsburgh, 1989, 5

Assists

Career: Wayne Gretzky, 260; Mark Messier, 186

Season: Wayne Gretzky, 31, 1988; Wayne Gretzky, 30, 1985

Series other than final: Rick Middleton, Boston, Division Final 1983, 14

Final Series: Wayne Gretzky, Edmonton, 1988, 10

Game: Mikko Leinonen, NY Rangers, 1982, 6; Wayne Gretzky, Edmonton, 1987, 6

Points

Career: Wayne Gretzky, 382

Season: Wayne Gretzky, Edmonton, 1985, 47

Series other than final: Rick Middleton, Boston, 1983, 19

Final Series: Wayne Gretzky, Edmonton, 1988, 13

Game: Patrick Sundstrom, New Jersey, 1988, 8; Mario Lemieux, Pittsburg, 1989, 8

Stanley Cup Finals

From 1918 to 1926, the cup winner was determined in a series between the NHL and PCHA champion. Since 1927, the NHL champion has won the Cup.

Year	Champion	Runner-up	Games
1999	Dallas	Buffalo	4-2
1998	Detroit	Washington	4-0
1997	Detroit	Philadelphia	4-0
1996	Colorado	Florida	4-0
1995	New Jersey	Detroit	4-0
1994	NY Rangers	Vancouver	4-3
1993	Montreal	Los Angeles	4-1
1992	Pittsburgh	Chicago	4-0
1991	Pittsburgh	Minncsota	4-2
1990	Edmonton	Boston	4-1
1989	Calgary	Montreal	4-2
1988	Edmonton	Boston	4-0
1987	Edmonton	Philadelphia	4-3
1986	Montreal	Calgary	4-1
1985	Edmonton	Philadelphia	4-1
1984	Edmonton	NY Islanders	4-1
1983	NY Islanders	Edmonton	4-0
1982	NY Islanders	Vancouver	4-0
1981	NY Islanders	Minnesota	4-1
1980	NY Islanders	Philadelphia	4-2
1979	Montreal	NY Rangers	4-1

Year	Champion	Runner-up	Games
1978	Montreal	Boston	4-2
1977	Montreal	Boston	4-0
1976	Montreal	Philadelphia	4-0
1975	Philadelphia	Buffalo	4-2
1974	Philadelphia	Boston	4-2
1973	Montreal	Chicago	4-2
1972	Boston	NY Rangers	4-2
1971	Montreal	Chicago	4-3
1970	Boston	St. Louis	4-0
1969	Montreal	St. Louis	4-0
1968	Montreal	St. Louis	4-0
1967	Toronto	Montreal	4-2
1966	Montreal	Detroit	4-2
1965	Montreal	Chicago	4-3
1964	Toronto	Detroit	4-3
1963	Toronto	Detroit	4-1
1962	Toronto	Chicago	4-2
1961	Chicago	Detroit	4-2
1960	Montreal	Toronto	4-0
1959	Montreal	Toronto	4-1
1958	Montreal	Boston	4-2
1957	Montreal	Boston	4-1
1956	Montreal	Detroit	4-1
1955	Detroit	Montreal	4-3
1954	Detroit	Montreal	4-3
1953	Montreal	Boston	4-1
1952	Detroit	Montreal	4-0
1951	Toronto	Montreal	4-1
1950	Detroit	NY Rangers	4-3
1949	Toronto	Detroit	4-0
1948	Toronto	Detroit	4-0
1947	Toronto	Montreal	4-2
1946	Montreal	Boston	4-1
1945	Toronto	Detroit	4-3
1944	Montreal	Chicago	4-0
1943	Detroit	Boston	4-0
1942	Toronto	Detroit	4-3
1941	Boston	Detroit	4-0
1940	NY Rangers	Toronto	4-2
1939	Boston	Toronto	4-1
1938	Chicago	Toronto	3-1
1937	Detroit	NY Rangers	3-2
1936	Detroit	Toronto	3-1
1935	Mtl. Maroons	Toronto	3-0
1934	Chicago	Detroit	3-1
1933	NY Rangers	Toronto	3-1
1932	Toronto	NY Rangers	3-0
1931	Montreal	Chicago	3-2
1930	Montreal	Boston	2-0
1929	Boston	NY Rangers	2-0
1928	NY Rangers	Mtl. Maroons	3-2
1927	Ottawa	Boston	2-0-2
1926	Mtl. Maroons	Victoria	3-1
1925	Victoria	Montreal	3-1

Year	Champion	Runner-up	Games
1924	Montreal	Van. Maroons	2-0
		Calgary Tigers	2-0
1923	Ottawa	Van. Maroons	3-1
		Edm. Eskimos	2-0
1922	Tor. St Patricks	Van. Millionaires	3-2
1921	Ottawa	Van. Millionaries	3-2
1920	Ottawa	Seattle	3-2
1919	*No champion; series between Montreal and Seattle halted because of flu epidemic.*		
1918	Tor. Arenas	Van. Millionares	3-2

Hockey Hall of Fame
Players

Names	Year Elected
Sid Abel	1969
Jack Adams	1959
Syl Apps	1961
George Armstrong	1975
Ace Bailey	1975
Dan Bain	1975
Hobey Baker	1945
Bill Barber	1990
Marty Barry	1965
Andy Bathgate	1978
Bobby Bauer	1996
Jean Beliveau	1972
Clint Benedict	1965
Doug Bentley	1964
Max Bentley	1966
Toe Blake	1966
Leo Boivin	1986
Dickie Boon	1952
Mike Bossy	1991
Butch Bouchard	1966
Frank Boucher	1958
George Boucher	1960
Johnny Bower	1976
Dubbie Bowie	1945
Frank Brimsek	1966
Punch Broadbent	1962
Turk Broda	1967
John Bucyk	1981
Billy Burch	1974
Harry Cameron	1962
Gerry Cheevers	1985
King Clancy	1958
Dit Clapper	1947
Bobby Clarke	1987
Sprague Cleghorn	1958
Neil Colville	1967
Charlie Conacher	1961
Lionel Conacher	1994

Names	Year Elected	Names	Year Elected
Roy Conacher	1998	Gordie Howe	1972
Alex Connell	1958	Syd Howe	1965
Bill Cook	1952	Harry Howell	1979
Bun Cook	1995	Bobby Hull	1983
Art Coulter	1974	Bouse Hutton	1962
Yvan Cournoyer	1982	Harry Hyland	1962
Bill Cowley	1968	Dick Irvin	1958
Rusty Crawford	1962	Buscher Jackson	1971
Jack Darragh	1962	Ching Johnson	1958
Scotty Davidson	1950	Ernie Johnson	1952
Hap Day	1961	Tom Johnson	1970
Alex Delvecchio	1977	Aurel Joliat	1947
Cy Denneny	1959	Duke Keats	1958
Marcel Dionne	1992	Red Kelly	1969
Gordie Drillon	1975	Ted Kennedy	1966
Graham Drinkwater	1950	Dave Keon	1986
Ken Dryden	1983	Elmer Lach	1966
Woody Dumart	1992	Guy Lafleur	1988
Tommy Dunderdale	1974	Newsy Lalonde	1950
Bill Durnan	1964	Jacques Laperriere	1987
Red Dutton	1958	Guy Lapointe	1993
Babe Dye	1970	Edgar Laprade	1993
Phil Esposito	1984	Jack Laviolette	1962
Tony Esposito	1988	Percy LeSueur	1961
Arthur Farrell	1965	Hughie Lehman	1958
Fernie Flaman	1990	Jacques Lemaire	1984
Frank Foyston	1958	Mario Lemieux	1997
Frank Fredrickson	1958	Herbie Lewis	1989
Bill Gadsby	1970	Ted Lindsay	1966
Bob Gainey	1992	Harry Lumley	1980
Chuck Gardiner	1945	Mickey MacKay	1952
Herb Gardiner	1958	Frank Mahovlich	1981
Jimmy Gardner	1962	Joe Malone	1950
Eddie Giacomin	1987	Sylvio Mantha	1960
Rod Gilbert	1982	Jack Marshall	1965
Billy Gilmour	1962	Fred Maxwell	1962
Moose Goheen	1952	Lanny McDonald	1992
Ebbie Goodfellow	1963	Frank McGee	1945
Michel Goulet	1998	Billy McGimsie	1962
Mike Grant	1950	George McNamara	1958
Shorty Green	1962	Stan Mikita	1983
Wayne Gretzky	1999	Dickie Moore	1974
Si Griffis	1950	Paddy Moran	1958
George Hainsworth	1961	Howie Morenz	1945
Glenn Hall	1975	Bill Mosienko	1965
Joe Hall	1961	Frank Nighbor	1947
Doug Harvey	1973	Reg Noble	1962
George Hay	1958	Buddy O'Connor	1988
Riley Hern	1962	Harry Oliver	1967
Bryan Hextall	1969	Bert Olmstead	1985
Hap Holmes	1972	Bobby Orr	1979
Tom Hooper	1962	Bernie Parent	1984
Red Horner	1965	Brad Park	1988
Tim Horton	1977	Lester Patrick	1947

Names	Year Elected
Lynn Patrick	1980
Gilbert Perrault	1990
Tom Phillips	1945
Pierre Pilote	1975
Didier Pitre	1962
Jacques Plante	1978
Denis Potvin	1991
Babe Pratt	1966
Joe Primeau	1963
Marcel Pronovost	1978
Bob Pulford	1991
Harvey Pulford	1945
Bill Quackenbush	1976
Frank Rankin	1961
Jean Ratelle	1985
Chuck Rayner	1973
Kenny Reardon	1966
Henri Richard	1979
Maurice Richard	1961
George Richardson	1950
Gordie Roberts	1971
Larry Robinson	1995
Art Ross	1945
Borje Salming	1996
Serge Savard	1986
Terry Sawchuk	1971
Fred Scanlan	1965
Milt Schmidt	1961
Sweeney Schriner	1962
Earl Seibert	1963
Oliver Seibert	1961
Eddie Shore	1947
Steve Shutt	1993
Babe Siebert	1964
Joe Simpson	1962
Darryl Sittler	1989
Alf Smith	1962
Billy Smith	1993
Clint Smith	1991
Hooley Smith	1972
Tommy Smith	1973
Allan Stanley	1981
Barney Stanley	1962
Peter Stastny	1998
Jack Stewart	1964
Nels Stewart	1962
Bruce Stuart	1961
Hod Stuart	1945
Cyclone Taylor	1947
Tiny Thompson	1959
Vladislav Tretiak	1989
Harry Trihey	1950
Bryan Trottier	1997
Norm Ullman	1982

Names	Year Elected
Georges Vezina	1945
Jack Walker	1960
Marty Walsh	1962
Harry 'Moose' Watson	1962
Harry Percival Watson	1994
Cooney Weiland	1971
Harry Westwick	1962
Fred Whitcroft	1962
Phat Wilson	1962
Gump Worsley	1980
Roy Worters	1969

Builders

Names	Year Elected
Charles Adams	1960
Weston Adams	1972
Frank Ahearn	1962
Bunny Ahearn	1977
Sir Montagu Allan	1945
Keith Allen	1992
Al Arbour	1996
Harold Ballard	1977
Father David Bauer	1989
J.P. Bickell	1978
Scotty Bowman	1991
George Brown	1961
Walter Brown	1962
Frank Buckland	1975
Jack Butterfield	1980
Frank Calder	1947
Angus Campbell	1964
Clarence Campbell	1966
Joseph Cattarinich	1977
Leo Dandurand	1963
Frank Dilio	1964
George Dudley	1958
James Dunn	1968
Emile Francis	1982
Jack Gibson	1976
Tommy Gorman	1963
Frank Griffiths	1993
Bill Hanley	1986
Charles Hay	1974
Jim Hendy	1968
Foster Hewitt	1965
W.A. Hewitt	1947
Fred Hume	1962
Punch Imlach	1984
Tommy Ivan	1974
William Jennings	1975
Bob Johnson	1992
Gordon Juckes	1979
John Kilpatrick	1960
Seymour Knox	1993

Names	Year Elected
Robert LeBel	1970
Al Leader	1969
Thomas Lockhart	1965
Paul Loicq	1961
John Mariucci	1985
Frank Mathers	1992
Frederic McLaughlin	1963
Jake Milford	1984
Sen. Hartland Molson	1973
Ian 'Scotty' Morrison	1999
Monsignor A. Murray	1998
Francis Nelson	1947
Bruce Norris	1969
James Norris	1962
James Norris Sr.	1958
William Northey	1947
J. Ambrose O'Brien	1962
Brian Francis O'Neill	1994
Frederick Page	1993
Frank Patrick	1958
Allen Pickard	1958
Rudy Pilous	1985
Norman 'Bud' Polie	1990
Sam Pollock	1978
Sen. Donat Raymond	1958
John Ross Robinson	1947
Claude Robinson	1947
Phillip Ross	1976
Gunther Sabetzki	1995
Glen Sather	1997
Frank Selke	1960
Harry Sinden	1983

Names	Year Elected
Frank Smith	1962
Conn Smythe	1958
Ed Snider	1988
Lord Stanley of Preston	1945
Capt. James Sutherland	1947
Anatoli Tarasov	1974
Bill Torry	1995
Lloyd Turner	1958
William Tutt	1978
Carl Voss	1974
Fred Waghorne	1961
Arthur Wirtz	1971
Bill Wirtz	1976
John A. Ziegler Jr.	1987

Referees and Linesmen

Names	Year Elected
Neil Armstrong	1991
John Ashley	1981
Bill Chadwick	1964
John D'Amico	1993
Chaucer Elliott	1961
George Hayes	1988
Bobby Hewitson	1963
Mickey Ion	1961
Matt Pavelich	1987
Mike Rodden	1962
Cooper Smeaton	1961
Red Storey	1967
Frank Udvari	1973
Andy Van Hellemond	1999

Notes

Introduction: From Canada to the World

1. Quoted in George Cantor and Anne Janette Johnson, *The Olympic Factbook*. Detroit: Visible Ink Press, 1997, p. 175.

Chapter 1: "Good Fun May Be Expected"

2. Quoted in Brian McFarlane, *History of Hockey*. Champaign, IL: Sports Publishing, 1997, p. 2.
3. Quoted in Glenn Weir, Jeff Chapman, and Travis Weir, *Ultimate Hockey*. Toronto: Stoddart, 1999, p. 5.
4. Quoted in Weir et al., *Ultimate Hockey*, p. 6.
5. Quoted in Weir et al., *Ultimate Hockey*, p. 8.
6. Quoted in McFarlane, *History of Hockey*, p. 6.

Chapter 2: "The Fastest Game in the World"

7. Quoted in Arthur Pincus, *The Official Illustrated NHL History*. Chicago: Triumph Books, 1999, p. 24.

8. Quoted in Dan Diamond, ed., *Total Hockey: The Official Encyclopedia of the National Hockey League*. Kansas City, MO: Andrews McMeel, 1998, p. 53.
9. Quoted in Pincus, *The Official Illustrated NHL History*, p. 33.
10. Quoted in Pincus, *The Official Illustrated NHL History*, p. 32.
11. Quoted in Diamond, *Total Hockey*, p. 16.
12. Quoted in McFarlane, *History of Hockey*, p. 42.
13. Quoted in Pincus, *The Official Illustrated NHL History*, p. 22.
14. Quoted in Pincus, *The Official Illustrated NHL History*, p. 45.
15. Quoted in Diamond, *Total Hockey*, p. 51.
16. Quoted in Weir et al., *Ultimate Hockey*, p. 209.

Chapter 3: Growing Pains and Great Hockey

17. Quoted in Pincus, *The Official Illustrated NHL History*, p. 63.
18. Quoted in Pincus, *The Official Illustrated NHL History*, p. 66.

19. Quoted in Brian McFarlane, *Stanley Cup Fever*. Toronto: Pagurian Press, 1978, p. 127.
20. Quoted in Pincus, *The Official Illustrated NHL History*, p. 193.
21. Quoted in Charles Wilkins, *Hockey: The Illustrated History*. New York: Doubleday, 1985, p. 32.
22. Quoted in Jim Coleman, Trent Frayne, Gare Joyce, and Jim Taylor, *Legends of Hockey*. Chicago: Triumph Books, 1996, p. 123.
23. Quoted in Zander Hollander, ed., *The Complete Encyclopedia of Hockey*. Detroit: Visible Ink Press, 1993, p. 24.
24. Quoted in Pincus, *The Official Illustrated NHL History*, p. 94.

Chapter 4: Challenge to Supremacy

25. Quoted in Diamond, *Total Hockey*, p. 63.
26. Quoted in Michael Ulmer, *The Top 100 NHL Hockey Players of All Time*. Toronto: McClelland & Stewart, 1998, p. 45.
27. Quoted in Hollander, *The Complete Encyclopedia of Hockey*, p. 213.
28. Quoted in Ulmer, *The Top 100 NHL Hockey Players of All Time*, p. 24.
29. Quoted in Pincus, *The Official Illustrated NHL History*, p. 133.
30. Quoted in Jack Batten, "The Return of Hockey's Proudest Warrior," *Maclean's*, January 23, 1965, p. 39.

Chapter 5: From the Broad Street Bullies to the Great One

31. Quoted in Pincus, *The Official Illustrated NHL History*, p. 134.
32. Quoted in Pincus, *The Official Illustrated NHL History*, p. 135.
33. Quoted in Pincus, *The Official Illustrated NHL History*, p. 182.
34. Quoted in Diamond, *Total Hockey*, p. 66.
35. Quoted in Ulmer, *The Top 100 NHL Hockey Players of All Time*, p. 18.
36. Quoted in Wilkins, *Hockey*, p. 37.
37. Quoted in Ulmer, *The Top 100 NHL Hockey Players of All Time*, p. 18.
38. Quoted in John Powers and Arthur C. Kaminsky, *One Goal: A Chronicle of the 1980 U.S. Olympic Hockey Team*. New York: Harper & Row, 1984, p. 209.

Chapter 6: "From a Redneck League to an International One"

39. Quoted in Diamond, *Total Hockey*, p. 69.
40. Quoted in Diamond, *Total Hockey*, p. 69.
41. Quoted in Diamond, *Total Hockey*, p. 70.
42. Quoted in Diamond, *Total Hockey*, p. 426.
43. Quoted in Diamond, *Total Hockey*, p. 427.

44. Quoted in McFarlane, *History of Hockey*, p. 257.

45. Quoted in Cantor and Johnson, *The Olympic Factbook*, pp. 176, 179.

46. Quoted in Diamond, *Total Hockey*, p. 484.

47. Quoted in Cantor and Johnson, *The Olympic Factbook*, p. 179.

48. Quoted in Diamond, *Total Hockey*, p. 484.

49. Quoted in Pincus, *The Official Illustrated NHL History*, p. 195.

For Further Reading

Caroline Arnold, *The Winter Olympics*. New York: Franklin Watts, 1993. This brief history highlights major events of the Winter Olympics, including a brief section on hockey.

Richard Beddoes, Stan Fischler, and Ira Gitler, *Hockey! The Story of the World's Fastest Sport*. New York: Macmillan, 1973. An examination of the NHL.

James Duplacey, *Hockey Superstars: Amazing Forwards*. New York: Morrow Junior Books, 1996. Duplacey presents the careers of great scorers, including Gordie Howe, Bobby and Brett Hull, Wayne Gretzky, and Maurice Richard.

———, *Hockey Superstars: Great Goalies*. New York: Morrow Junior Books, 1996. Another in the author's series depicting life in the NHL, this time featuring goalies such as Ken Dryden and Grant Fuhr.

———, *Hockey Superstars: Top Rookies*. New York: Morrow Junior Books, 1996. This is a fine collection of short biographies on the NHL's most promising young players.

Stan Fischler, *Hockey's Greatest Teams*. Chicago: Henry Regnery, 1973. Fischler provides a valuable resource on early NHL teams, written in an easy style.

Bill Gutman, *Roller Hockey*. Minneapolis: Capstone Press, 1995. Gutman presents the basics of roller hockey, also called in-line hockey.

John Martin, *In-Line Skating*. Minneapolis: Capstone Press, 1994. Covers the basics of the rapidly growing sport of in-line skating, and includes material about in-line hockey.

Cam Millar, *Roller Hockey*. New York: Sterling, 1996. Millar includes numerous photographs in his presentation of roller hockey, which covers how to play the game, which equipment is needed, and the basic rules.

Carrie L. Muskrat, *The Composite Guide to Hockey*. Philadelphia: Chelsea House, 1998. Muskrat's clear style of writing helps present the material in simple fashion.

Frank Orr, *The Stanley Cup*. New York: G. P. Putnam's Sons, 1976. Orr describes each of the Stanley Cups up to the 1970s. This is a good place to start for younger fans interested in learning about the postseason playoffs.

John Sias, *Kids' Book of Hockey*. Secaucus, NJ: Citadel Press, 1997. Sias focuses on the rules and how to play the game, including a chapter on hockey's history.

Works Consulted

Jack Batten, "The Return of Hockey's Proudest Warrior," *Maclean's*, January 23, 1965. Batten presents a look at the career of Ted Lindsay, who was instrumental in organizing the NHL players into a union.

George Cantor and Anne Janette Johnson, *The Olympic Factbook*. Detroit: Visible Ink Press, 1997. A valuable source of information on any sport that has appeared in the Winter Olympics. The authors sprinkle short biographies of key athletes throughout their text.

Jim Coleman, Trent Frayne, Gare Joyce, and Jim Taylor, *Legends of Hockey*. Chicago: Triumph Books, 1996. A fine pictorial history of the game's top stars, completed with the cooperation of the Hockey Hall of Fame.

Dan Diamond, ed., *Total Hockey: The Official Encyclopedia of the National Hockey League*. Kansas City, MO: Andrews McMeel, 1998. A comprehensive look at the National Hockey League from its inception through the 1990s. Abundant statistics and records complement a fine series of introductory chapters explaining the sport's growth.

Dan Diamond and Joseph Romain, *Hockey Hall of Fame*. New York: Doubleday, 1988. The authors produce a history of the NHL as seen through the lives of its great stars. The volume is filled with helpful information.

Ken Dryden, *The Game*. New York: Times Books, 1983. Dryden, one of the most intelligent players to enter the NHL, delivers a thoughtful and thought-provoking depiction of his life in the league.

Stan Fischler, *Cracked Ice: An Insider's Look at the NHL*. Chicago: Masters Press, 1999. Longtime hockey writer and commentator Fischler examines the key issues of hockey, including owner-player strife and administration of the NHL.

Stan Fischler and Shirley Walton Fischler, *The Hockey Encyclopedia*. New York: Macmillan, 1983. The Fischlers produce a compilation of hockey facts, records, and profiles. Most valuable is an introductory chapter covering the history of hockey.

Zander Hollander, ed., *The Complete Encyclopedia of Hockey.* Detroit: Visible Ink Press, 1993. Hollander's eighteen chapters include, among other items, team histories, player biographies, a history of the NHL, memorable moments, and statistics. This book is very helpful to the serious researcher or to the casual fan.

Douglas Hunter, *Champions: The Illustrated History of Hockey's Greatest Dynasties.* Chicago: Triumph Books, 1997. The writer presents an NHL history that emphasizes the contributions made by important teams through the years. He includes the 1950s Detroit Red Wings and the 1980s New York Islanders among his nine teams.

————, *Scotty Bowman: A Life in Hockey.* Chicago: Triumph Books, 1998. A biography of one of the greatest NHL coaches. Hunter includes much material on the Montreal and Detroit teams.

Brian McFarlane, *History of Hockey.* Champaign, IL: Sports Publishing, 1997. McFarlane's history divides the NHL year by year and presents the material in short paragraph form. While it gives much information, it is difficult to present themes and trends through the years in this type of layout.

————, *Stanley Cup Fever.* Toronto: Pagurian Press, 1978. Hockey historian McFarlane looks at the postseason playoffs. A solid account of the Stanley Cup.

Frank Orr, *Hockey's Greatest Stars.* New York: G. P. Putnam's Sons, 1970. Though an older book, it contains helpful material on some of hockey's legends.

Arthur Pincus, *The Official Illustrated NHL History.* Chicago: Triumph Books, 1999. This is one of the best books at gaining a picture of the NHL's history. Pincus fills it with excellent stories and gripping quotes.

John Powers and Arthur C. Kaminsky, *One Goal: A Chronicle of the 1980 U.S. Olympic Hockey Team.* New York: Harper & Row, 1984. The authors deliver a strong book about the amazing 1980 hockey team. They include many quotes from team members, coaches, and observers in this compelling volume.

Michael Ulmer, *The Top 100 NHL Hockey Players of All Time.* Toronto: McClelland & Stewart, 1998. Ulmer gives brief biographies of the hundred most important NHL players, from Wayne Gretzky (#1) to Frank Nighbor (#100), who played from 1917 to 1930.

Glenn Weir, Jeff Chapman, and Travis Weir, *Ultimate Hockey.* Toronto: Stoddart, 1999. A lighthearted look at the NHL that includes a vast amount of interesting material and player information. A great book for understanding the human element of the sport.

Charles Wilkins, *Hockey: The Illustrated History.* New York: Doubleday, 1985. An account of hockey's history. Numerous pictures and quotes enliven the text.

Index

Picture Credits

About the Author

John F. Wukovits is a junior high school teacher and writer from Trenton, Michigan, who specializes in history and biographies. Besides biographies of Anne Frank, Jim Carrey, Colin Powell, and Martin Luther King Jr. for Lucent, he has written biographies of the World War II commander Admiral Clifton Sprague, Barry Sanders, Tim Allen, Jack Nicklaus, Vince Lombardi, and Wyatt Earp. A graduate of the University of Notre Dame, Wukovits is the father of three daughters—Amy, Julie, and Karen.